Carol Kuijer

MW01411470

SPIRITUAL DEVELOPMENT WORKBOOK 101

(PLUS BONUS SECTIONS FOR PSYCHICS & PSYCHIC MEDIUMS)

BY SUE M. SWANK, PSYCHIC MEDIUM

TABLE OF CONTENTS

DEDICATION

I want to say clearly right here that everybody has the same abilities as psychics and psychic mediums. The difference here is that many have not acknowledged or explored their abilities ***(this is most often due to social/religious/family influences).***

Having said the above statement, I wish to personally dedicate this workbook to those exploring their spirituality and to those who are curious, but wish to learn from the shadows.

"Faith sees the invisible, believes the unbelievable and receives the impossible" - Corrie Ten Boom

HOW TO USE THIS MANUAL

This manual is very basic and is designed to flow smoothly by providing the information first and then the chapter test follows after each segment.

The tests are self-tests and to be used as a self-gauging tool ***(FAIR WARNING: in order for you to answer some test question within this book must be researched on your own. This is to challenge & encourage your learning upon the subject)***, which will allow you to see where ***(if any)*** you ***(the reader/student)*** need to apply extra effort in understanding and applying the information provided within this manual.

The bonus section is provided directly to psychics & psychic mediums. In this section, I ***(the author)*** share some of my opinions & experiences, in an effort to "bring to light" certain topics and situations that you ***(reader/student)*** may interact with at some point.

Best Wishes Always...

Sue M. Swank, Psychic Medium

CHAPTER #1

- What is Spiritualism?
- History of Spiritualism
- 7 Basic Principals of Spiritualism
- Types of Spiritualisms ***(Part 1)***
- Spiritualism & Society
- Spiritualism vs. Organized Religion ***(what's the difference?)***
- CHAPTER #1 TEST

WHAT IS SPIRITUALISM?

Spiritualism is the practice of establishing communication between the living and those who have crossed over. It is within itself a universal religion that centers around the belief that those whom are mediums have the ability to send and receive messages from those within the spirit world itself. It is a natural, innate ability that lies within all of mankind (***some have it to a higher degree than others***).

HISTORY OF SPIRITUALISM

Spiritual communication is thought to have existed since mankind itself. Native tribes ***(Mayans, Native/Caribbean, Etc.)*** would communicate with those who have crossed over through way of spirit quests, sweat huts, etc. The same can be said about the Greeks, Romans, Etc. It has even been believed that Jesus himself was a psychic medium, as well as a healer and teacher (***as was John the Baptist***).

Two of the most prominent scholars ***(and influential)*** in the 18th century were Emmanuel Swedenborg (1688-1722) & Andrew Davis Jackson (1826-1910).

The writings and works from Sweden scientist & astronomer, Emmanuel Swedenborg, were translated to him via spirits ***(as he, himself had previously reported)***. He believed that he was brought to the spirit world by Jesus to learn the higher, spiritual truths.

Andrew Davis Jackson was considered to be the "John the Baptist" of spiritualism. Not only was he a spiritualist author ***(one of the most respected during his time)***, he was also Clairvoyant & heard voices. Even as a child growing up, he was able to enter a trance like state and communicate with those who within the spirit world.

In 1847, Mr. Jackson stated that it the afterlife would soon be proven.

It was a year later (1848) that the Fox Sisters became widely known for their spiritual encounters during séances. This moved spiritualism into the modern era, where it has continued to gain in popularity, as well as been extensively studied by many.

7 BASIC PRINICPALS OF SPIRITUALISM

- The fatherhood of God ***(the belief in a higher source)***
- The brotherhood of man ***(the belief that mankind is a unified collective soul. We are ALL spiritually connected)***
- The Communion of Spirits and the Ministry of Angels ***(the belief that spirits and Angels gather together to share messages to those who are still living)***
- The Continuous Existence of the human soul ***(the belief that man's soul lives on indefinitely throughout all lifespans and realms)***
- Personal Responsibility ***(the understanding of one's behavior and the impact of our actions)***
- Compensation and Retribution hereafter for all the good or evil deeds done on earth ***(the belief in karma)***
- Eternal Progress open to every human soul ***(the belief that each soul continues to ascend to it's highest level)***

TYPES OF SPIRITUALISM, PART #1

- Clairvoyance: The Medium can see spirit
- Clairaudience: The Medium can hear spirit
- Clairsentience: The Medium can feel and sense spirit
- Trance Mediumship: Spirit comes through the Medium ***(Medium talks and acts like the spirit)***
- Transfiguration: A mask appears in-front of the Mediums face of the spirit. The medium looks like the spirit

- Automatic Writing: The Medium allows spirit to use their hand and arm to write with
- Automatic Drawing: The Medium allows spirit to use their hand and arm to draw with

SPIRITUALISM & SOCIETY

Modern society ***(as a whole)*** can be categorized into 2 areas:

- The Believers ***(those who identify with a structured faith based religion & those who believe in a higher power and identify themselves as simply "spiritual")***
- The NON-Believers ***(those who elect to believe that there is no higher power, no afterlife, etc.)***

Now when you include those who have the ability to communicate with the souls, who have crossed over, the "Believers" category becomes more divided.

In some faith based religions, the communication between the living and those who have crossed over is often looked upon as taboo, disrespectful and dangerous.

When one says they are a medium ***(person who communicates with those who have crossed over)***, they almost become a sector amongst themselves.

This is because many of those within the organized, faith based religions tend to look upon mediums with disbelief, as well as accusing them ***(again in some instances, but certainly not all)*** of breaking some sort of commandment.

When it comes to those who are non-believers, they are steadfast within their beliefs that there is no higher power, no afterlife, nothing. To them, a person laying claim to be a medium is considered ***(more often than not)*** to be mentally ill, delusional, etc.

Over the years, Spiritualism itself has begun to be more widely accepted. Each day, each year, the struggle to prove the existence of the afterlife seems to fade a bit more, as reports come to light that substantiates the claims from mediums world-wide, who have communicated with those who have crossed over.

But even though spiritualism in itself an innate, natural ability within all of us, is still not as widely accepted as it should be.

It begs to ask here, that if one believes in a "higher power" and that "Angels" & the "Holy Spirit" can come down to protect, to deliver "divine messages", etc. then why is it so hard to also believe in the fact that a person, a living breathing soul from a higher power, can also communicate with those who have crossed over?

SPIRITUALISM VS. ORGANIZED RELIGION
(WHAT'S THE DIFFERENCE?)

As it has been said before, spiritualism is the universal belief that there are those who can effectively communicate with those who have crossed over in ***(both)*** a receptive, as well as projective manner ***(in other words they can send & receive messages from those in the afterlife)***.

<u>There are 3 beliefs in spiritualism:</u>

- Those who have crossed over want to maintain their communication with the living
- The afterlife, or "spirit world", is seen by Spiritualists
- That spirits are capable of providing useful knowledge about moral and ethical issues, as well as about the nature of God

Organized religion is the belief in a faith structured set of rules ***(commandments to some)***, that was created by one supreme god figure. They have a clear set of rules/commandments that dictate how mankind should live their life. Should one fail to abide by these rules/commandments, punishment is swift and ***(sometimes)*** eternal.

Overall, they tend to shun those who are capable of communicating with those who have crossed over. In the eyes of many, those who do communicate with those in the afterlife is actually communicating with Satan himself and is set to be forever dammed in an eternal hell.

However, over the course of the years, modern views have branched off of the previous stricter religious point of views ***(in some areas and churches)*** to where now, one can be into spiritualism, as well as follow a specific organized religion path.

TEST FOR CHAPTER #1

1. What is a natural, innate ability that lies within all of mankind?

2. Who was considered to be "John the Baptist" of spiritualism?

   Andrew Jackson

3. In 1848, the Fox sisters became widely known for what?

   moving Spiritualism into the modern era

4. What was the name of the Fox Sisters ghost?

5. Give examples of each of the 7 types of spiritualisms:

6 • What does Spiritualism mean to you?

7 • Pick one (1) organized religious path ***(can be any you chose)***, write down their similarities to Spiritualism, and then write down their differences:

8 • What are 3 beliefs in spiritualism?

9 • Modern society can be divided into what 2 categories?

10 - One of the 7 principals of spiritualism states that "Eternal Progress open to every human soul ***(the belief that each soul continues to ascend to it's highest level)***", do you agree with this statement and why? ***(Please explain thoroughly)***:

CHAPTER #2

- Types Of Spiritualisms ***(Part 2/further discussion on identifying with your primary)***
- Spiritualism & You ***(when does it begin? Where does it come from? How do you work with it?)***
- Utilizing Your 5 Tools ***(What are your 5 tools & how do you use them?)***
- Tapping Into Your Energy Source ***(meditation/breathing/grounding/etc.)***
- Opening The Door To The Other Realms ***(The 4 Basic Realms)***
- Keeping A Spiritual Journey Journal ***(the importance of keeping a journal during the first year of development)***
- CHAPTER #2 TEST

TYPES OF SPRITUALISMS
(PART #2/IDENTIFYING WITH YOUR PRIMARY)

Test to gauge your ability:

- How often do you "sense" energy around you? Often___ Sometimes___ Rare___
- How often do you get impressions/feelings from objects? Often___ Sometimes___ Rare___
- Did you ever daydream as a child? Yes___ No___
- How often do you remember your dreams? Often___ Sometimes___ Rare___
- Do you dream vividly? Yes___ No___
- After you dream, have often have you ever:
- Recalled a certain smell or smells? Often___ Sometimes___ Rare___
- Recalled a certain sensation/touch/feel? Often___ Sometimes___ Rare___
- Felt a lingering presence around you? Often___ Sometimes___ Rare___
- Are you able to eat at a crowded restaurant? Yes___ No___
- Are you able to sense other people's emotions? Often___ Sometimes___ Rare___
- Do you have a hard time sleeping and/or keeping a regular sleep routine? Often___ Sometimes___ Rare___
- How often do you feel "drained" by other people's drama/chaos? Often___ Sometimes___ Rare___
- When you try to connect with spirits, please number which senses become active 1rst, 2nd, 3rd, 4th, 5th, & 6th? Sight___ Sense___ Smell___ Taste___ Touch___ Hear___
- When you first meet someone, what is the first thing you notice about them? Energy/presence___ Eye/Facial expression___ Body language___ Sound of their voice___
- How often do you go to another place in your mind when you meditate? Often___ Sometimes___ Rare___

- Have you ever heard a voice or whispers around you when you are quiet? Yes___ No___
- Have you ever seen glimpses of shadows/figures from the corner of your eyes when you are quiet? Yes___ No___

Telepathy:

Telepathy is the ability to read thoughts, usually surface thoughts. Telepathy is fairly common to some degree. The most common type is between close family or friends and manifests as answering questions before they are asked, knowing when a family member is thinking of you, or thinking about them and they call.

Slightly less common is the ability to read the surface thoughts of strangers. Even less common is being able to read the deep or subconscious thoughts of people, friends, family or anyone else. It is not, however, completely unknown. If you have the disconcerting habit of knowing everything about a person when you meet them, you are at least a highly gifted telepath. In crowds this may manifest as "white noise" or constant buzzing in the ears (brain), accompanied by a feeling of pressure on the brain.

This is due to the constant noise of all of the thoughts of others that one is unable to block. Many highly gifted telepaths are unable to live in highly populated areas, and an apartment complex is a nightmare. They are also prone to intense headaches. This gift may or may not be related to proximity. For strangers, it is usual that the person must be close by (though not always the case). Family seems to be instantly accessible, due to the non-local nature of the gift, speed of light laws do not apply. Strong thought, as in a disaster or violent attack, may be picked up without prior knowledge of the person at all, if they are in the vicinity or there are enough people concentrating on mentally screaming at the top of their lungs.

This gift also manifests more strongly if one really desires something (a strong focus of will or emotion). To block out the noise, shielding must be practiced constantly, and the person should put up permanent shields around their home.

To develop this gift, one should focus on an individual and relax, allowing whatever impressions one is receiving to come through. Write them down. This is best developed with close friends or family.

Telepathy can manifest in three ways. A sending telepath cannot "hear" the thoughts of others, but instead broadcasts his/her own thoughts to anyone even remotely sensitive.

A ***sending telepath*** can influence others, without being aware of it, by strongly desiring something.

A danger is that one who is a sending telepath, without any of the other gifts, has a tendency to be self-centered and demanding, and petulant when they don't get their way.

A ***receiving telepath*** can "hear" but can't send, others don't pick up their thoughts. This person might believe the voices, thoughts, or impressions of ideas to be internally generated, and might doubt his/her sanity. As is often the case, the thoughts are incongruous, and seem to come from nowhere, but the individual cannot distinguish the internal thought from the external.

Most common is one who can both send and receive, and the response is usually enough to convince the person that s/he is not crazy, though the gift might be hidden out of a fear of being unusual, especially if the person's church mistakenly equates the gifts with possession.

The "voices" or impressions gathered by the telepath are relaying accurate, verifiable information based on the consensual hallucination we call reality. Ask. The information is usually pretty mundane, and the telepath, upon thinking about it, can learn to tell that the thought did not originate in his/her own brain (for example: "I need to remember the ice cream" when the individual is allergic to ice cream and is talking to someone on his way to the store.)

If one is hearing voices counseling them to murder or warning that the toaster is influencing our thoughts by controlling the television, then some mental health care is definitely in order.

Empathy:

Empathy is similar to Telepathy but revolves around emotions instead of thoughts. Empathic ability can also manifest in sending, receiving, or both.

A ***sending empath*** may not have much sense of what others feel, because the can usually change an unpleasant response into a more favorable one.

The ***receiving empath*** is in danger of being swamped by the feelings of others, and may not know whether the feeling is internally or externally generated. To be an empath is to be able to sense what others are feeling, and influence what others are feeling is the most common manifestation. This may or may not occur along with telepathy.

If one is an empath, feelings and emotional atmosphere play a strong part in every aspect of one's life. Crowds are almost unbearable. The individual may feel angry/depressed/elated/in love/enraged in a matter of a few moments as the gift ranges out and picks up whatever is there.

A feeling of being on a roller coaster and of smothering in a sea of feelings may accompany this. On the other hand, the person seems to gravitate to the individual in the room who needs help dealing with an emotional problem.

An empath makes an excellent counselor and is usually the one to whom friends bring their problems because "s/he really understands."

Psychometry:

Psychometry is the ability to pick up images, histories, and impressions from objects and places, by holding an abject, like a sweater or a ring; one Sees or senses information about the owner or most frequent user of the object. This Gift is usually combined with one or more of the "***Clair***" Gifts.

Precognition:

The ability to sense, see, and /or hear things that may happen in the future. Usually combined with one of the other Gifts. Sometimes manifests in dreams that come true, visions, flashes, hunches, or just "knowing".

Retrocogniton:

The ability to see, sense, and/or hear things that happened in the past. Same description as above. Also increases the likelihood of "***seeing***" past lives and connections with others.

Telekinesis:

The ability to move object with the mind. Once thought rare, this gift usually manifests in adolescents going through puberty and is responsible for about 95% of the poltergeist phenomena. This Gift can also manifest disguised as "the Klutz", someone who, usually when emotionally stimulated, objects around them fall over, break, etc. ***(they walk by the table but do not touch it, yet something spills)***.

PyroKinesis:

This is the "Firestarter", the ability to light and/or control fire or heat with the mind. This also tends to manifest with strong emotion. The firestarter may often not be conscious of their gift, but will have a history of fires happening around them ***(The kitchen when they were a child, a house down the street, etc.)*** Do not confuse this with pyromania! The Gifted person needs to learn to direct heat into the earth, as holding it in can cause damage. Concentration and emotional balance are essential.

SPIRITUALISM & YOU (WHEN DOES IT BEGIN? WHERE DOES IT COME FROM? HOW DO YOU WORK WITH IT?)

Spiritualism is born within us. It comes from a higher source of power. In order to work with spiritualism, you need to have an open mind and the willingness to communicate with those who have crossed over into the afterlife.

Spiritualism is centered around energy ***(sending/receiving messages with those who have crossed over, getting vibrations/images/etc. from objects and/or pictures, etc.).***

Each human body has what is known as Chakras. Chakras are energy centers. Although most people have heard of seven chakras, there are actually 114 in the body. The human body is a complex energy form; in addition to the 114 chakras, it also has 72,000 "nadis," or energy channels, along which vital energy, or "prana," moves

Your Chakras have a lot to do with your gifts overall ***(especially your Third eye & Crown Chakra)***.

In order to work with your gifts & expand your abilities, your chakras need to be open and free of blockage ***(this is also true for general well-being overall)***.

As a person begins their journey to understand their gifts & abilities, they then begin the task of unblocking their Chakras ***(especially their Third eye & their Crown Chakra, where communication with those who have crossed over primarily comes from)***.

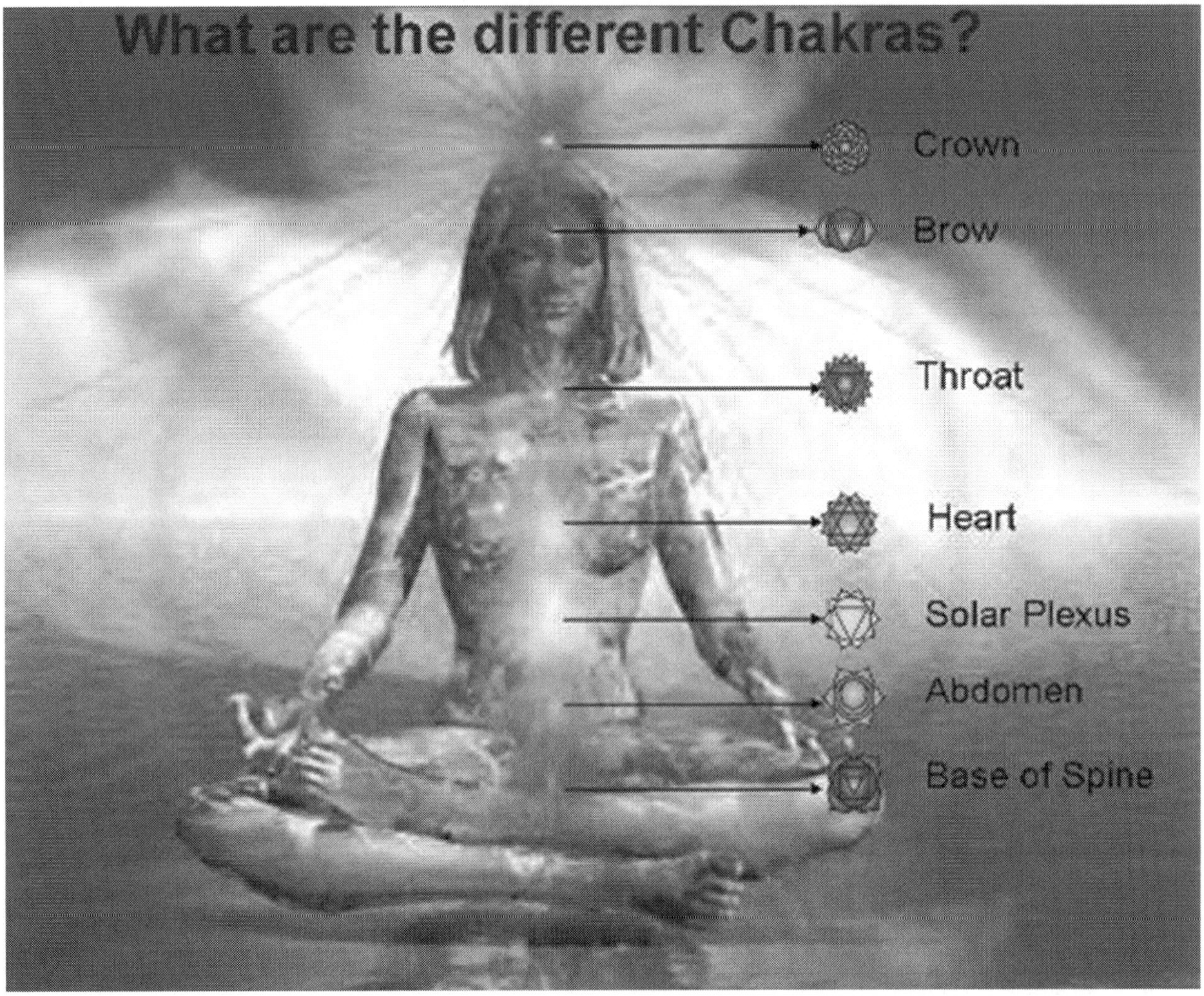

- ***Root Chakra*** - Represents our foundation and feeling of being grounded.
    - Location: Base of spine in tailbone area.
    - Emotional issues: Survival issues such as financial independence, money, and food.
- ***Sacral (Spenlic) Chakra*** - Our connection and ability to accept others and new experiences.
    - Location: Lower abdomen, about 2 inches below the navel and 2 inches in.
    - Emotional issues: Sense of abundance, well-being, pleasure, sexuality.
- ***Solar Plexus Chakr***a - Our ability to be confident and in-control of our lives.
    - Location: Upper abdomen in the stomach area.
    - Emotional issues: Self-worth, self-confidence, self-esteem.
- ***Heart Chakra*** - Our ability to love.

    - Location: Center of chest just above heart.
    - Emotional issues: Love, joy, inner peace.
- ***Throat Chakra*** - Our ability to communicate.
    - Location: Throat.
    - Emotional issues: Communication, self-expression of feelings, the truth.
- ***Third Eye Chakra*** - Our ability to focus on and see the big picture.
    - Location: Forehead between the eyes. ***(Also called the Brow Chakra)***
    - Emotional issues: Intuition, imagination, wisdom, ability to think and make decisions.
- ***Crown Chakra*** – The highest Chakra represents our ability to be fully connected spiritually.
    - Location: The very top of the head.
    - Emotional issues: Inner and outer beauty, our connection to spirituality, pure bliss.

The best way to open your Chakras is by meditation.

UTILIZING YOUR 6 TOOLS
(WHAT ARE YOUR 6 TOOLS & HOW DO YOU USE THEM?)

As you begin your path to spiritualism, you will discover that within you are 6 basic tools that will become quite active on your journey:

- Sight ***(for those who are primarily Clairvoyant, etc.)***
- Sound ***(for those who are Clairaudient, etc.)***
- Sense ***(when you can sense the energy & spirits around you)***
- Taste ***(Sometimes while working with spirits and/or your guides, etc. you will be introduced to different tastes, whether good or bad)***
- Smell ***(Sometimes while working with spirits and/or your guides, etc. you will also encounter different smells)***
- Touch ***(sometimes while working with spirit, you will encounter those who actually touch you)***

TAPPING INTO YOUR ENERGY SOURCE
(MEDITATION/BREATHING/GROUNDING, ETC.)

Tapping into your energy source & unblocking your Chakras is conducted through meditation. Meditation is a great way to connect with your higher spirituality, as well as ground & centering yourself overall.

Relaxation technique for meditations:

- Get into a comfortable position ***(please sure be to wear comfortable clothing)***.
- Close both your eyes and your mind to everything.
- Begin to take a few deep breathes allowing a brief pause between inhaling and exhaling ***(in through your nose, pause, out through your mouth, pause. Repeat)***.
- Feel the tension flowing from your body and mind, as your limbs begin to relax.
- Visualize a color you find pleasant ***(some prefer blue)*** gently circle around you.
- At this point, some may experience a slight tingling sensation, don't tense up. Allow it flow through your body.
- Relax your mind. Visualize the stress and worries from your day be removed each time you exhale through your mouth.
- Relax your heart. Visualize the negative feelings and unwanted memories being removed with each exhale through your mouth.
- Relax your soul. With each breath, feel the pulse and rhythm of your heartbeat. Let it guide you to a sacred place in your mind that you have visualized.
- Visualized a sacred place ***(some visualize themselves lying under stars; some visualize a quiet beach, etc.)***.
- Allow your mind to get detailed ***(actively involve all 5 of your senses)*** and creative when visualizing your sacred place. This is your sanctuary.

- While in your sanctuary, mentally give yourself positive affirmations ***(I love myself and others, I am a good person, I forgive myself and others who has crossed me. I am in the right place and time for my needs, etc.)***
- Allow yourself to linger there for a while longer. Re-supplying your body and spirit with energy.
- Slowly, allow yourself to come back to your surroundings.
- Allow yourself to be completely quiet for a few minutes while your eyes and mind focus back

OPENING THE DOOR TO THE 4 THE OTHER REALMS
(THE 4 BASIC REALMS)

- The physical realm is composed of comparatively dense, slowly vibrating matter and energies. Our own vast physical universe with its many stars and galaxies is little more than a handful of sand along an endless, cosmic beach.
- The quantum realm is a buffer zone between the physical and astral worlds. From our perspective here on Earth, it is a place to tie up loose ends after we die and prepare to move on to paradise. It has also become a rather troubled place.
- The astral realm is a place of form and structure much like our own physical world, though the structures and activities in the astral realm are more malleable—adapting more smoothly to the thoughts and intentions of the astral residents, who include most people who once had lived here on Earth.
- The ethereal realm is a formless world, consisting of pure consciousness of its ethereal inhabitants, who exchange information more efficiently and in greater quantity than the supercomputers of our world.

How can you access these realms and communicate with those who have crossed over, as well as other energies?

- Dreams ***(In many cases, many of us are already accessing these realms through our dreams. This is because during our sleep mode, our minds are free and clear of clutter and other "society inhibitions", thus enabling us to***

explore these realms, learn lessons, get advice and/or other spiritual nudges, etc.)

- Meditation ***(Meditation is another excellent method to open the doors to those realms as well)***

Now as you begin to work more and more with your abilities and gifts, the more open you will be overall to communicate with spirits.

KEEPING A SPIRITUAL JOURNEY JOURNAL (THE IMPORTANCE OF KEEPING A JOURNAL DURING THE FIRST YEAR OF DEVELOPMENT)

During the first year of your spiritual development, your whole mind/spirit/body will begin to experience changes. You will literally start to ***FEEL*** quite different. This is because your chakras as opening up, and becoming more receptive to communication with spirits and energies around you.

Some of the possible side effects are:

- Slight buzzing/ringing in your ears ***(almost like a white noise)***
- Your body becomes more sensitive to touch and sensations ***(you begin to notice a difference in fabrics, etc.)***
- Your sight and hearing become heightened ***(this is often due to your third eye Chakra becoming unblocked)***
- Your sleep may be disturbed for a while ***(this is because you are opening yourself up to outside energies overall)***
- You feel a slight tingling/vibration ***(especially in your third eye area)***

It is during this initial period of awakening, where keeping a journal is important.

Here are some reasons why:

- Assist with organizing your thoughts

- Assist you to see where you are going
- Gives you inspiration
- Can assist you in calming down, thus becoming more centered the more you write

It is also good to review your journal every 4 weeks. After a year, leave it for a month or two to give yourself a breather. After the breather, pick up your journal and read from the beginning and more often than not, you will find some interesting revelations about yourself.

<u>What should you write in your journal? Here are some ideas:</u>

- Dreams
- Visions
- Reflective memories ***(more often than not, as we begin our spiritual journey, we become more reflective about our own past and the memories connected with them)***
- Inspirational quotes that call out to you

TEST FOR CHAPTER #2

- Explain the 3 types of Telepathy:

- What is Psychometry?

- What is an Empath? Explain the 3 types of Empaths:

- What Gift can also manifest disguised as "the Klutz"? What ***(usually)*** happens around them?

- How many Chakras are in the human body overall?

- List & explain the 7 main Chakras ***(their location, their color and their emotional uses)***:

- What are the 2 main Chakras that have the most to do with your spirituality & explain why?

- Explain each of the 4 Realms and how to get there:

- List the 5 ***(possible)*** side effects that you can experience during your first year on your spiritual journey:

- List the 4 reasons as to why it is important to keep a spiritual journey journal:

******FROM THIS SESSION ON, YOU WILL BE REQUIRED TO CREATE & MAINTAIN A SPIRITUAL JOURNEY JOURNAL******

CHAPTER #3

- Acknowledging The Changes In You Overall ***(senses heightened, vivid dreams, sensitivity levels, etc.)***

- The Importance Of Balancing Yourself for Overall Well Being

- Incorporating Outside Tools To Connect With The Other Side ***(a breakdown of Crystals, Tarot, Ouija, Pendulums, music, incense, candles, pictures & objects)***

- Preparing Yourself For The Connection ***(basic preparation steps)***

- Meeting Your Guides ***(who, what are they & how to meet them)***

- Meeting Your Animal Spirit Guides ***(how many? what types? What are their roles?)***

- CHAPTER #3 TEST

ACKNOWLEDING THE CHANGES IN YOU OVERALL *(SENSES HEIGHTENED, VIVID DREAMS, SENSITIVITY LEVELS, ETC.)*

As you begin to awaken and development your abilities, you will begin to notice some changes happening within your body.

Such as:

- Difficulty in sleeping ***(or unable to achieve a restful sleep)***
- Eating binges ***(craving for sugary and/or salty foods)***
- Ears ringing/vibrating/hearing whispers, etc.
- Vivid dreaming
- More highs/lows in energy ***(one minute burst of energy, then drained completely)***
- Sense of smell & taste can become more acute
- Feel as if you are not alone in a room when you are
- More sensitive to other peoples energy/tone of voice/mannerisms, etc.

The best way to get through this is to try and create a set schedule as much as possible, along with giving yourself adequate “down time” to relax from everything.

Meditation & Reiki are excellent tools to assist you in alleviating some of these extreme changes.

THE IMPORTANCE OF BALANCING YOURSELF FOR OVERALL WELL BEING

As you begin to learn about your gifts and actively work with them, you will begin to notice your own body & spirit sending you signals when it needs a break. The first series of signals can be:

- Mild headache
- Feeling sluggish

- Not feeling as if you get enough sleep
- Minor digestive issues

Now, if and when ***(and most likely when, because when become passionate about something, it is human nature for us to completely lose ourselves within it for a while, almost like a passion overload)*** we ignore those signals, our bodies and spirits THEN begin to send harsher signals:

- Nagging headache ***(migraine level at times)***
- Lack of appetite/unhealthy eating habits ***(binge junk food eater)***
- Moderate to severe sleep related issues, not sleeping well, restless sleep
- Easily irritable and shows signs of impatience/frustration/feelings of being "over whelmed"
- Unable to process conversations in general/forgets things easily/distracted
- ***(Sometimes)*** Flu like symptoms, achy, feeling "off balance", lethargic, etc.

It is vital that you understand what your body and spirit ***(not the outside spirits but rather the one inside of you LOL!)*** is trying to relay to you. It is important to always important to give back to yourself and replenish yourself on a daily basis. This is a must ***(especially if you are just opening yourself up to working with energies)***.

Some of the best ways to do this is:

- Taking a brief 10 minute walk ***(not a speed walk, but more of a relaxing walk around your block, look at things outside, clear your mind, leave that list of things back at the house and don't think about it while you are on your walk)***.
- Cut off everything electronic in your home about 15 minutes prior to going to bed and listen to the silence. Enjoy the silence. Take it in. It ***(the silence)*** has a way of assisting in healing your soul after a long day ***(believe it or not)***.
- Take at least one meal a day, and enjoy it. Enjoy the textures, the taste, if you cook, enjoy that process of making it by hand. Take your time with it ***(don't rush, this is your time to enjoy this meal)***

- Exhale as you get settled in bed at night and close your eyes ***(exhaling is a way of telling your mind and body "Ok this is enough for right now")***
- Find something "***fun***" to do every day for 10 minutes ***(great way to find your inner child)***
- Sprinkle lavender scented baby powder on your mattress just prior to placing fresh sheets on your bed, also place your clean sheet set in your freezer for an hour before placing them on the bed, then make the bed tight. Later, when you get into your bed, you smell the lavender, feels the softness from the baby powder, mixed with the slight coolness of the sheets ***(this is an excellent way to ease yourself back into a peaceful sleep)***.
- Get Reiki once a month and meditate when possible ***(even if for a few moments a day or every other day)***

It is important to stress the fact of overall well-being, both spiritually and psychically. Your spirituality is connected to your overall well-being on a very intimate level. If you are unbalanced, and/or running low on your own resources, then your Chakras become clogged, thus creating a blockage within your spirituality path.

INCORPORATING OUTSIDE TOOLS TO CONNECT WITH THE OTHER SIDE

(A BREAKDOWN OF CRYSTALS, TAROT, OUIJA, PENDULUMS, MUSIC, INCENSE, CANDLES, PICTURES & OBJECTS)

When you wish to establish a line of communication with those who have crossed over, the main tool ***(and strongest)*** tool you should have ready is your mind. However there are some other tools which can be of some use, should you desire to incorporate them as well. They are:

- Crystals
- Tarot/Pendulums/Ouija
- Music
- Incense/Candles

- Pictures/Objects

<u>All crystals and rocks vibrate on different levels and come in 2 forms:</u>

- Rough ***(natural)*** cut ***(as is from the earth they were dug up from)***
- Polished ***(by man or machine in most cases)***

It is a personal preference as to whether you chose rough cut or polished when it comes to your crystals. What is important is how they react and feel to you when you are near them and/or hold ***(touch)*** them.

A "***Jack of All Trades***" in crystals is the "Quartz Crystal". The Quartz Crystal can act like a grounder, communicator, amplifier, and receiver of energy.

<u>Tarot decks</u> have been around for centuries and can provide for a good base for connecting with those who have crossed over, as well as displaying a possible doorway to future events, etc.

Tarot decks come in all shapes, sizes and styles. The different spreads start with the basic 3 card pull to the most complicated ***(utilizing 2 or more decks during a reading)***.

When choosing a tarot deck for your personal use, take your time. Hold each deck as they call out to you. Be sure to close your eyes and listen with your heart, feel the energy from the deck and see if it works well with your own energy. If it does then great, you have a new deck. If it doesn't, put it down and move on to the next deck that calls out to you.

<u>Pendulums</u> are also known as dowsing rods in some cases. They are usually crystal or metal objects, at the bottom of a chain and/or string. They work by way of your vibrational energy and that of the energy around them. They respond to yes or no questions. Some mediums have been known to use them during sessions ***(especially if the energy is that of a child or the energy is freshly crossed over)***.

<u>Ouija Boards</u> have been around for quite some time and usually have a bad reputation attached to them ***(a friend of a friend of a friend who knew this person who used a Ouija Board and they were possessed by some demon and went on a***

killing spree then killed themselves, etc.), when in all reality, the Ouija board was actually designed to communicate with those who have crossed over ***(as well as possessing the ability to connect with entities from other realm as well sometimes)***. As with ***ANY*** tool, it is always recommended that you research the tool first to see if you want to use it, then enquire from those who have used that tool ***(from both sides, the positive results and the negative results)*** **THEN** sit down and explore your personal feelings about possibly using this tool and if you feel that it would help you to achieve your highest spiritual level by using it. But understand that to every "***bad legend***" running amuck, there is usually some version of truth hidden somewhere.

Music has been around since cave man basically. It soothes the soul, inspires creativity, as well as provoking emotions from deep within us. Music can be used with meditation to assist in going to your sacred space, and/or to other realms. Even singing a Mantra ***(a repetitive word or phrase over and over and over***) can be useful in achieving a higher vibrational level.

Incense/Candles assist in opening up 2 of your senses ***(sight and smell)***. They can serve as a focus point during your meditation, as well as when you enter trance mediumship work.

Pictures/Objects are usually tied with Psychometry ***(the reading of history or of a spirit via images, objects such as jewelry, clothing, etc.)***. Many psychic mediums find looking at an image of a specific person creates an easier pathway to connecting to that specific spirit.

PREPARING YOURSSELF FOR THE SPIRITUAL CONNECTION *(BASIC STEPS)*

Before you decide to open that line of communication with spirit or spirits, you must make sure that you are:

- Well rested
- Not hungry or distracted

Prior to attempting to connect with a spirit ***(or spirits)***, there are 4 basic steps that you must follow first:

- Ground yourself ***(plant your feet directly on the ground/floor, allowing the energy to flow through you, etc.)***
- Create a shield ***(this is an imaginary bubble or circle that surrounds you. Protecting you from unwanted energies, etc.)***
- Meditate ***(this is where you start to open the line of communication between yourself and the spirit realm)***
- Call upon your guides to assist you in sending/receiving messages from those who have crossed over

MEETING YOUR GUIDES
(WHO, WHAT ARE THEY & HOW TO MEET THEM)

Your guides have been with you since your creation. They were assigned to you for numerous reasons. They assist in advising you during difficult times, they help enlighten you on your life's path, they also soothe you during the not so good periods in your life. Bottom line, your guides give you strength.

<u>Each person has 3 types of guides:</u>

- Soul Guides: Some refer to them as "Your inner voice". They are actually part of your soul. Your soul existed before you were born. When it was decided that you would be reborn ***(in many instances)*** or simply born into your current existence, part of your soul stayed behind to learn lessons, while "your inner voice" guide tagged along, guiding you, advising you, keep you company, etc. They are most like you, because they are you. They will stick with you during your entire journey.
- Time Guides: These guides will ***(sometimes)*** appear themselves to you via other people ***(stranger in passing who gives you some really good advice when you need it the most, offer you assistance in some way, etc.)***. They help. That's their sole job. To assist you during a specific period of time.

Then once that task is completed, they are gone. But the lesson, assistance, etc. stays with you.

- Ancestral Guides: Ancestral guides are those within your blood line. They could be that great grandmother 3 times removed, whom you have never met before, and/or a recent parent who has passed over, etc. They pop in and out during various periods, to offer guidance as needed. Often they assist in keeping you within the connected with the family ways ***(whether you know it or not)***.

It is possible to have more than one guide with you ***(yes it can get a little crowded at times)***. Communicating with your guides is as simple as clearing your mind and listening to them.

The best way to meet your guides is through the following 2 methods:

- Meditation ***(Go to your sacred space, get comfortable, ask for them to appear in front of you and give you their names and their roles in your life)***
- Dreams ***(prior to going to sleep, ask your guides to communicate with you through your dreams and tell you about themselves, etc.)***

MEETING YOUR ANIMAL SPIRIT GUIDES
(HOW MANY? WHAT TYPES? WHAT ARE THEIR ROLES?)

Animal guides are perhaps the most special in many instances. These spiritual guides will enter your dreams, they will appear in physical form, etc. When they do, you instantly feel a connection. ***(Sometimes)*** that instant connection is so intense, it can bring tears to your eyes. It can be a humbling experience.

Their job is to guide by showing you their ways of behavior, how they live, how they interact, etc. They can also deliver messages to you from the other side in your dreams, etc.

A person may have several animal spirit guides in and out of their lives ***(sometimes all at once, other times they come in one by one)***

******NOTE: It is possible to have a mythological animal as a guide, as well as a real one******

TEST FOR CHAPTER #3

- Name 5 changes that can occur within your body while your gifts and abilities are developing:

  ____
  ____
  ____
  ____
  ____

- List some ways which can help you to alleviate some of these changes:

  ____
  ____
  ____
  ____
  ____

- Explain WHY it is important for you to balance yourself while on your spiritual path:

  ____
  ____
  ____
  ____
  ____

- In reading some ways that you can replenish your body and spirit, what are some ***OTHER*** ways ***YOU*** ***(personally)*** can think of that could be of beneficial to help you replenish your body and spirit:

  ____
  ____
  ____

- Name the one strongest tool you already have when it comes to working your spiritual path:

- Name the crystal that is the "***Jack of all trades***" & explain what it does ***(this will involve you researching this)***:

- What 2 tools are tied with Psychometry and how do they work?

- What 2 senses are most active with what 2 tools?

- What does creating a shield do for you?

- What are Time Guides and explain their role:

- Explain the 2 methods in which you can meet your spirit guides:

- What is the role of an animal spirit guide?

- How can you meet your animal spirit guide?

____

____

- List YOUR spirit guides and explain what category they fall in ***(for example: Ancestor/time/soul/etc.)***:

  ____

  ____

  ____

  ____

  ____

- List & describe ***<u>YOUR</u>*** animal spirit guides:

  ____

  ____

  ____

  ____

  ____

****NOTE****

For those of you whom have not met your spirit guides and/or your animal spirit guides, now is a good time to seek them out (mediation and/or dream).

Focus all of your energies on meeting them so you can answer #14 & #15

CHAPTER #4

- Psychics, Psychic-Mediums, & Mediums ***(differences, similarities, etc.)***
- Self-Exploration As A Medium ***(how far do you want to go as a medium? Setting your goals, etc.)***
- Mediumship & The Paranormal ***(being asked to join a team, what to expect, etc.)***
- Taking Care Of Yourself ***(replenishing your well)***
- Coming Out As A Medium ***(pros & cons of disclosing to others, handling the skeptics, etc.)***
- Establishing Healthy Boundaries ***(in both spiritual & physical realms)***
- CHAPTER #4 TEST

PSYCHICS, PSYCHIC MEDIUMS, & MEDIUMS
(DIFFERENCES, SIMILARITIES, ETC.)

As you begin to develop your spirituality, your path will enlighten you as to which category you belong to. Discovering where you fit in isn't always easy or simple. There will be moments where you think you might fit in a certain area, only to discover that you really belong ***(thrive better and stronger***) in a different area.

While there are numerous books to choose from for educational purposes, hands on experience and working with your guides is often proven to be far more beneficial in the long run.

There are 3 types of spiritualists:

- Psychics
- Psychic mediums
- Mediums

Psychics are sensitive to the energies around them and have the ability to receive visions, impressions, etc. from their surroundings. They are most often quite versed in psychometry, precognition & retrocognition. They are greatly tuned into their inner world and have a solid control over their emotions (for the most part). Overall they can process these energies faster and in numerous ways.

Psychic mediums are sensitive to the energies & spirits around them, as well as in other realms. They can also establish communication with those who have crossed over into the afterlife. Psychic mediums are often versed in clairaudience ***(hearing)***, clairvoyance ***(clear seeing)***, clairsentience ***(clear sensing)***, as well as empathy.

Mediums have the ability to connect with energies & spirits in the afterlife. They can often receive messages from those who have crossed over through clairaudience ***(hearing)***, clairvoyance ***(clear seeing)***, clairsentience ***(clear sensing)***.

SELF-EXPLORATION AS A MEDIUM
(HOW FAR DO YOU WANT TO GO AS A MEDIUM? SETTING YOUR GOALS, ETC.)

There comes a time in your spirituality discovery, where you stop and ask yourself "How far do I want to go with this?", "What do I want to do with my abilities?" These are questions that only you can answer for yourself ***(with the assistance of your guides)***.

(Usually) There are 3 categories, in which many place themselves in:

- Simply to learn ***(this is where they simply have a desire to learn about their own spirituality, as well as spirituality in general and they leave it at that***)
- It turns into a "spiritual hobby" for them ***(this is where they use their abilities to read for friends/family/people for whom they are close to, etc.)*** This is something that is self-pleasuring ***(meaning they do not charge overall)***
- It is a new career path ***(whether it is their first career choice, their second career choice or third, etc.)***. They make it a point to learn as much as they can about their gifts and abilities, to them it is a serious study, one that is never ending. They make it a point to not only learn about their spirituality, but learn the business side of spirituality and begin to treat it as their business

MEDIUMSHIP & THE PARANORMAL
(BEING ASKED TO JOIN A TEAM, WHAT TO EXPECT, ETC.)

Mediumship is the communication between the living and those who have passed over to the afterlife. ***They (the ones who have crossed over to the afterlife) communicate with us in various ways:***

- Through other people
- Through signs ***(smells, sounds, dreams, etc.)***

Paranormal is basically a generic catch all word for those who have and/or are experiencing paranormal events around them ***(and sometimes to them as well)***. This includes encounters with poltergeist, spirits, entities, angels, demons, etc.

A paranormal team is comprised of individuals ***(from various backgrounds)***, who join together and conduct a scientific investigation, in hopes of recording valid proof that the afterlife and the supernatural does exist.

In many instances, psychics and/or psychic mediums are included with the team. ***<u>A typical example of a paranormal team investigating a reported haunting may go like this:</u>***

- The team leader and the psychic medium will initially go out to location first to do a walk through and conduct interviews, etc. During this time, the psychic medium walks through ***(with the team leader)*** the location, explaining what they get ***(briefly)*** energy wise from the area ***(this is done with no equipment)***
- Upon returning, they sit down with their notes, ***(with the rest of the team members)*** and discuss everything. If all goes well, an appointment is then scheduled to conduct a full investigation ***(majority of paranormal investigations are conducted at night)***

Now...on the evening of the investigation, the psychic medium will ***(again)*** walk through the location in one of 2 fashions:

- The psychic medium will walk through the location with one of more team members and some equipment ***(video recorder, audio recorder, EMF, EVP recorder, etc.)***, then exit so a full scientific investigation can then take place
- The psychic medium joins the entire team during the investigation and assist by relaying messages, etc.

Upon completion of the investigation, all data is reviewed ***(along with the findings from the psychic medium)*** and follow up meeting is scheduled to discuss the evidence, make referrals, etc.

TAKING CARE OF YOURSELF *(REPLENISHING YOUR WELL)*

While walking your spirituality path, it is important to find balance between the spirit realm and the physical realm. Each day it is vital that you try to maintain the following:

- A healthy diet ***(that also includes high energy foods to help avoid burn out)***
- Plenty of sleep/down time ***(if your Melatonin is off balance then your sleep pattern can be disrupted, thus throwing the rest of your routine/schedule out of whack)***
- Laughter ***(seriously, finding humor and laughing daily can actually assist in reducing your stress levels, which can assist in your immune system and overall mental/emotional/physical well-being)***
- Exercise ***(even if it is for a brief walk around your block, or you park a few blocks away from your work or the store, etc. it simply works to help get your blood flowing)***

Each of these can assist in keeping your chakras functioning at top speed, which can help you find balance.

COMING OUT AS A MEDIUM
(PROS & CONS OF DISCLOSING TO OTHERS, HANDLING SKEPTICSM ETC.)

There comes a point in nearly every psychic medium stops and asks themselves "when should I come out as a psychic medium?" This isn't an easy, black and white answer by far. There is a great deal to consider before making that announcement to your friends and family and to the public in general, such as:

- Your job/career
- Your spouse/partner job/career
- Your personal religious connections ***(church, etc.)***
- Your friends/family

The pro side is that everyone accepts you as a psychic medium and life goes on as normal. The con side is that you stand the chance at being ridiculed, possibly lose some business ***(if you own your own business)***, your spouse/partner and children can get teased at work/school. As for religious connections, either they will embrace it and your gifts or turn their backs on you for whatever reasons they deem fit.

When it comes to your friends and family, no doubt you will have at least one or two that will flat out refuse to accept anything you talk about when it comes to your gifts. It then comes down to you and how far you want to include them when it comes to your spirituality path.

Those who support you, will also assist you in flourishing in your spirituality. Those who do not support you will drain your energy if you fail to establish a healthy boundary.

A skeptic is defined as a person who questions the validity or authenticity of something purporting to be factual. Quite simply, they chose not to believe in something for whatever reason, even when the proof is over whelming factual.

As a psychic medium, you will no doubt encounter one or two or a herd of them. So what do you do when you encounter a skeptic? Do you argue your side till blue in the face? No that would only fan the flames and end the end would give you ***(and others around you)*** a headache. Do you present "factual evidence" to prove those from the otherside can and often do communicate with us in the living? No. Why? Simple, they would simply elect not to believe it from you. So then how do you get around a skeptic?

First, respect their point of views. Nobody said you have to agree ***(or even like them)*** with them. But you do have to respect them.

Second, you embrace their skeptism. You also take the time right then and there to accept the reality that until they choose that they are ready and open to accept the fact that those from the other side can and often do communicate with the living, there is very little to nothing at all that can be done to flip that switch.

No “magic reading” from Uncle Henry will change that either until the person themselves make that decision.

<u>Now, there are 2 basically types of skeptics that you, as a psychic medium will encounter:</u>

- Those who live strictly in the scientific world ***(basically all these guys want is 100% scientific proof, that was scientifically conducted in a scientifically controlled environment, over a course of years and factual scientific case studies are not only proven, but well documented in books and Universities)***
  And/or...
- Those who want a reading, get a reading, get solid proof during the reading and will still say “Nope. Nope. Nope.”, only then to go outside to their cars, to call their best friend and, not only talk about how awesome the reading was, but how factual it was.

Having a skeptic around you is actually healthy. They assist in keeping you grounded and more aware of your gifts, as a psychic medium. They will force you to evaluate yourself and the messages which you receive and pass on to others. They will force you to step back sometimes and become a skeptic on yourself and others, who also share your gifts.

Your job is not to change them or their thought patterns/beliefs, or even to attempt to “***WOW***” them with a profound reading, etc. But to understand that they are simply not ready to accept your version of reality and the color of your sky.

Now if, by chance, they do come around to your line of thinking and are receptive to believing in your gifts or others like you, then that is pure gravy. But if not, don’t get upset, don’t engage in debate, and don’t try to sway them over to your side.

But embrace them. Acknowledge their right to have their opinions and respect their right to have their opinions and keep being true to yourself and your guides.

ESTABLISHING HEALTHY BOUNDARIES AS A MEDIUM
(IN BOTH SPIRITUAL & PHYSICAL REALMS)

There comes a time in your experiences as a medium where you encounter 3 types of profound experiences:

- You are unable to go to a certain place, because you feel as if you are being over-crowded and/or pulled in a hundred different directions ***(tons of chatter, chaos, etc.)***
- You become the token "doctor at the cocktail party" with someone/group of people (they call/text/etc. you constantly with every little bump that happens in the night, they think they are haunted ***(or possessed)*** and only you can help soothe their nerves, they ask you endless questions about their future/their family members ***(dead and alive)/their health/etc.)***.
- Spirits from the other-side seem to invade your space 24/7 ***(trust me it can happen)***.

When any of the above 3 incidents occur ***(or all 3 of them)***, Your body and psyche start giving you signals:

- Headaches ***(anywhere from dull/mild ache to a full blown migraine throb)***
- Losing patience quickly ***(your tolerance level greatly decreases)***
- Feeling over-whelmed
- Physical pain ***(eyes hurt, muscle ache, etc.)***
- Sleepy/exhausted ***(feeling as if you can just crawl into bed and sleep the rest of the day away, etc.)***
- Wanting to be "left alone to sit quietly for a while"

The solution is to establish boundaries and stick to them.

The ***first experience*** ***(entering a certain place and feeling over-crowded, being pulled into a hundred different directions, etc.)*** can and does occur ***(even to the most experienced, the most shielded, the most grounded, etc.)***.

The best way to resolve that is:

- To acknowledge that a certain place or places will have a certain effect on you
- Limit your time in that certain place
- Have a distraction for you ***(a book, music, a game, etc.)***
- After being at that certain place, go for a soothing/peaceful walk outside in nature ***(if you can tolerate it and if weather permits, go barefoot, it helps you ground back to the earth and the sensation of the grass not only stimulates your feet, but feels soothing overall)***
- Upon returning home, grab a hot shower and change your clothing ***(the energy from that area can attach to you, so make sure you wash them before wearing them again)***

The ***second experience*** is becoming the token "doctor at a cocktail party" occurs when your well-meaning friends/family members get excited to learn that you are a medium and they come to you with every little incident, every question, at all hours of the day & night. They also invite you over all the time or to lunch with their other friends and introduce you as "This is my friend, she/he can talk to the dead! Go on! Ask them about someone who died!"

As well-meaning as they are and as close as the two of you may be, if this is allowed to continue, you will feel as if you are only wanted because of you being a medium ***(and thus, places the relationship in danger)***.

The best and only way to resolve this is to sit them down and discuss this with love and honestly ***(but most of all be clear)***.

Establish basic rules/guidelines ***(for the sake of the relationship)*** that work for the both of you and doesn't impede the relationship or your being a medium.

The ***third and final experience*** deals directly with spirits who bombard you 24/7. They are in your dreams, they are in the front part of your mind, you can hear them, you can see them, you can feel them.

The reason this happens is because when you first become open to the other side, it is as if the flood gates open up and your mind is open, constantly processing information. This is actually pretty normal (again everyone goes through this at one time or another).

The best way to deal with this situation is by two ways:

- Incorporate your guides and tell them to assist in blocking them during certain times ***(sleeping, personal time, etc.)***
- Telling those from the other-side to "Stop", "Go Away", "Not Right Now!" ***(visualize you hanging a "Closed" sign during certain times and leave it until you are ready to "open" for business again)***

Establishing healthy boundaries is vital for a healthy, fulfilling life overall ***(whether it is spiritual, non-spiritual, etc.)*** By establishing healthy boundaries ***(and sticking to them)***, you will soon discover that chaotic situations/people/etc. will cease in time.

CHAPTER #4 TEST

- In your own words, explain the difference between psychic, psychic medium and a medium:

  ____
  ____
  ____
  ____
  ____

- Name a famous person know as a psychic, explain who they are and how they use their psychic abilities:

  ____
  ____
  ____
  ____
  ____

- Name a famous person known as a psychic medium, explain who they are and how they use their abilities:

  ____
  ____
  ____
  ____
  ____

- Name a famous person known as a medium, explain who they are and how they use their abilities:

  ____
  ____
  ____

- What are the 3 categories spiritualists usually fall into:

- In your own words, describe what category ***YOU*** would place yourself in and what ***YOUR*** goal is as a psychic medium:

- What is mediumship:

- In your own words, name two ways in which communication is established between spirits and a medium:

- Explain the benefits of daily laughter:

____

____

____

____

____

- List 2 famous psychic mediums or mediums, who have joined paranormal T.V. teams, and the names of their teams:

____

____

____

____

____

- List the pros & cons of ***<u>YOU</u>*** coming out as a psychic medium/medium:

____

____

____

____

____

- In your own words, describe the 2 types of skeptics:

____

____

____

____

____

- How would ***<u>YOU</u>*** handle a skeptic:

____

____

____

- Name a benefit that a skeptic provides:

- Name one of the most famous skeptics of psychic abilities and describe their views in your own words:

- Why is it important to establish and maintain healthy boundaries:

- Explain the 2 methods in which you can create boundaries with spirits:

CHAPTER #5

- Famous Psychic Mediums & Mediums
- Developing Your Own Style ***(what works best for you personally & basic guidelines)***
- Reading For Others ***(gauging their comfort level, how to relay messages, should you charge? Enlisting the assistance of your guides in readings, turning down the chatter)***
- Dealing With Unpleasant Images/Smells/Sensations/Etc.
- The Importance of A Digital Recorder During Sessions
- Hitchhikers From The Other Side ***(who are they & how to get rid of them)***
- CHAPTER #5 TEST

?

FAMOUS PSYCHICS & MEDIUMS

When it comes to psychic mediums, the list is endless ***(from the world famous to those whose names nobody will probably ever know of except in small circles).***

Some of the most well known for their gifts and abilities are as follows:

- John Edward
- Theresa Caputo
- Noreen Reiner
- Lisa Williams
- Allison DuBois
- Edgar Cayce
- James Van Praugh

DEVELOPING YOUR OWN STYLE (WHAT WORKS BEST FOR YOU PERSONALITY WISE & BASIC GUIDELINES)

At first, many try to mimic those whom they respect the most within the world of psychic mediums. While there is nothing wrong this this, there comes a point to where you need to step out of their shadow and claim your own identity.

Developing your own style, while you are walking your spiritual path is essential to your reputation and image as a psychic medium.

While creating your own style, you need to ask yourself these questions about your personality:

- What is my personality like overall in public ***(as compared to being with friends/family? What is my personality when I am alone?)***
- Am I a "touchy/feely" person ***(enjoys hugs, touches, showing affection, etc.)***

- How do I handle emotions ***(do I try to avoid them and become logical, do I become emotional as well? Etc.)***
- How do I like information given to me ***(straight forward, sugar coated, etc.)***
- How do I speak to people ***(direct, indirect, etc.)***
- Do I have patience with people

Once you have figured out your personality levels, you need to figure out how they work into these basic guidelines:

- Show respect to the client ***(they have come to you for very sensitive and personal reasons. They deserve the respect.)***
- Show compassion and understand ***(no matter the reason they came to you, or the questions they ask, understand that they need your compassion and understanding to assist them through whatever situation they are going through during that time. Try to spend a few extra moments with them after your session, to let them know they are important and valued as a person.)***
- Do not ever tell them what to do ***(as psychic mediums, it is important to understand that we are not here to tell anyone what to do, however we can guide, offer suggestions, options, etc. the goal though is for them to figure out what works best for them, not you)***
- Do not ever give out medical advice ***(unless you are a licensed medical professional, you are not trained to give out medical advice on any level, so therefore do not do so, under ANY circumstance)***
- Always maintain a strong level of confidentiality ***(this helps in your clients to feel safe in sharing themselves with you, also strengthens your reputation as a psychic medium. Overall just solid business practice)***

READING FOR OTHERS

(GAUGING THEIR COMFORT LEVEL, HOW TO RELAY MESSAGES, SHOULD YOU CHARGE? ENLISTING THE ASSISTANCE OF YOUR GUIDES IN READINGS, TURNING DOWN THE CHATTER)

Prior to reading a client ***(or friend/family member)***, it is important that you be able to recognize their body language. Understanding their body language can actually assist you in relaying whatever messages from the afterlife in a more efficient and caring mannerism.

Some of the key points to look for are as follows:

- Are their hands tightly clasped together? Are the fingers tightly curled up within the hand itself? Are their hands sweaty? Can you see the whites of their knuckles? Are they fiddling with something ***(ring, watch, etc.?)***, are they sitting on their hands?
- Are their arms crossed protectively in front of them? Rigid?
- How are their feet? Are they pointed towards you or pointed off to the side or curled around the chair?
- Are they performing self-pacifying movements with their hands ***(stroking their throat, or their playing with their hair, etc.)***?
- How is the tone of their voice? Strained, high pitched, shaky, etc.
- How is their breathing rate? Quick & shallow?
- How is their eye contact with you? Are they making eye contact? Looking away ***(floor, etc.)***?
- Are they nibbling on their lips, picking at a bump/sore, etc.?

If you notice any of these behaviors, then proceed with caution ***(usually these behaviors are an indicator of feeling nervous, scared, uncertain, vulnerable, etc.)***. Be mindful in how you relay messages to them during the session ***(no matter how well you may know them)***.

Understand that they may be nervous because this is their first psychic medium experience, or maybe they could be conflicted with their religious beliefs, etc.

The main thing for you to do is listen. Listen to the messages given to you from those who have crossed over, and listen to the client in front of you.

DEALING WITH UNPLEASANT IMAGES/SMELLS/SENSATIONS, ETC.

During your psychic mediumship experience, you will ***(no doubt)*** at some point come across a session where you encounter unpleasant events such as:

- Violent/graphic images
- Offensive smells/odors
- Uncomfortable sensations ***(icky feelings, being held down, etc.)***

When these come to you in way of messages, it is important that you understand that you are receiving these for a reason. The main thing to keep in mind is to NOT over react to them.

Open communication with your client is important here (especially when it comes to situations such as these.

Another way to deal with these unpleasant experiences is to remind yourself that it has nothing to do with you. Separate yourself from it if you must ***(while still being present for the reading)***.

THE IMPORTANCE OF A DIGITAL RECORDER DURING SESSIONS

As you begin to perform readings, many start out simply writing everything down, then putting everything in an email and sending it to the client. While this is a good practice overall, sometimes vital points and messages get lost in translation.

The use of a digital recorder during sessions is ***(usually)*** the preferred method of recording sessions.

The process is simple:

- You start by stating your name, your clients name, as well as the date & time of the session

- You record the session in it's entirely
- As you end the session, you state the end time of the session
- You go home, download the recording to your computer, then provide a link of it to your client via email

Some psychic mediums prefer to keep their clients links in files for a certain period of time ***(in case of follow up sessions, etc.)***.

Doing readings in this fashion ensures your client that they have everything from the session ***(many times clients will not understand a message until much later, so the digital recording of their session is actually beneficial for them)***.

HITCHHIKERS FROM THE OTHER SIDE
(WHO ARE THEY & HOW TO GET RID OF THEM)

As you become more familiar with your readings, and strengthen your connection to those who have crossed over, you will eventually pick up some extra energies here and there. These are called "***hitchhikers***".

Sometimes during readings, ***(or even while at places like the cemetery, hospital, a funeral/funeral home, during paranormal investigation, etc.)***, the left over energies ***(whether pleasant or unpleasant)*** can attach themselves to you.

This happens for a variety of reasons:

- They are not finished giving you messages
- You have not cut the connection cord from them
- You are connected in one way or another to someone they are bonded with
- There are ways to tell if you have "hitchhikers" attached to you:
- You feel "crowded"
- You feel as if a thick layer of grease or "ick" is covering you
- You feel "uncomfortable"
- The best way to remove them is by the following after session:
- Shower ***(while you visualize cutting the cords from the attachments)***

- Change into ***FRESH*** clothing
- Nibble on a light meal
- Ground
- Meditate
- Ask your guides to assist you in removing the attached energies
- Shield

Be sure to re-shield after removing the attachments. This is important to ensure that they will not return.

STEPS IN READING IMAGES & OBJECTS

As a psychic medium, there will be times when you are requested to read images and/or objects.

While this can ***(sometimes)*** be intimidating for both the novice psychic medium, as well as the seasoned psychic medium, it can also be quite beneficial for everyone involved.

The following guidelines are advised and can be of use:

- Utilize your guides when reading the image and/or holding the object
- Close your eyes and clear your mind, allowing information to be given to you
- Give yourself time to properly receive the information
- Write down the information and details which you are receiving
- Do not discount anything ***(feeling, sensations, smells, voices, etc.)***
- Be sure to separate your personal feelings from what you are receiving

Remember that energy is active within the image and/or object. What you are receiving is the energy impressions. Your guides can assist you in understanding this energy itself.

More often than not, you will receive images and messages from those who have crossed over connected to the image and/or object that you are working on.

It is important to closely listen to these spirits. They are connected to the image and/or object for a reason ***(whether they are in the image, or connected to the person in the image or were a previous owner of whatever object you are holding at that time)***.

For those who are Empaths ***(both projecting and receiving)***, reading images and/or objects can be both daunting and exhilarating.

The key point to remember if you are an Empath is for you to shield yourself and take extra time to process what you are getting, as well as separating your own feelings, etc.

<u>On a side note:</u> If you are an Empath, take extra care when purchasing jewelry from antique shops, flea markets, even new jewelry from stores. The residual energy left on the object(s) and/or spirits that may or may not be connected to the item can throw you into a whirlwind of questions. And emotions, It has been suggested that proper and thorough cleanings of the items can performed prior to wearing them or having them in your home.

<u>Some of the methods to do this is as follows:</u>

- Set them out in direct moonlight for a few hours
- Cleanse them in gentle soapy water, then let air dry and smudge later
- Leave in freezer overnight

In general, reading images and/or objects can offer you a mixture of flashes and emotions such as:

- Happiness/sadness
- Fear/anger
- Confusion
- Sexual feelings ***(sometimes)***

Also in some cases, certain smells can come forth, for example:

- Smell of home baked cookies or any meal if an elderly woman ***(or any person really)*** used to own a certain object or is in the image or connected to the person in the image
- Flowers, perfume, gasoline ***(from automobiles and motorcycles)***, etc.
- Geographical smells such as woods, seascapes ***(beach)***, field of flowers/meadows, etc.

Sometimes all of these flashes, sensations, smells, sounds, etc. can hit you at once. The key point is to remain calm, allow yourself a few extra moments to process the information and separate your own emotions, etc.

CHAPTER #5 TEST

- Research & write a brief summary about EACH of the 6 psychic mediums that were mentioned:

  ____

  ____

  ____

  ____

  ____

- Describe your personality style for relaying messages between spirit & client:

  ____

  ____

  ____

  ____

  ____

- List 2 basic guidelines which you ***FEEL*** are the most important and explain WHY they are most important to you:

  ____

  ____

  ____

  ____

  ____

- Name 3 key points in gauging a clients' body language that you ***(personally)*** would notice first and explain why:

  ____

  ____

  ____

- What is the main thing for you to do as a psychic medium & explain why:

- Explain ***(in your own words)*** how ***<u>YOU</u>*** would handle offensive smells/images/etc. during a session:

- Explain ***(in your own words)*** why a digital recorder should be used ***(explain for both the medium and the client)***:

- Explain what hitchhikers are and how to recognize them, as well as some ways to remove them:

- Explain ***(in your own words)*** how you can remove residual energy from objects:

____

____

____

____

____

BONUS SECTIONS FOR PSYCHICS & PSYCHIC MEDIUMS

- SPIRITUAL AWAKENING
- STEP AWAY FROM THAT SPIRIT!
- DIFFERENCE BETWEEN READING FACES & READING SPIRITS
- DEALING WITH EMOTIONS DURING READINGS
- DEBRIEFING AFTER A SESSION ***(ESPECIALLY AN INTENSE SESSION)***
- RECOGNISING & REMOVING EGO ***(Ego + messages = disaster)***
- POINTS TO REMEMBER FOR GIVING ONLINE READINGS
- UNEXPECTED TRANCES
- WHEN TO SHARE SENSITIVE INFORMATION
- THE IMPORTANCE OF CONTINUOUS SPIRITUAL EDUCATION
- PSYCHICS & THE LAW

SPIRITUAL AWAKENING

A spiritual awakening can occur at different stages during a person's life. Sometimes it can occur during traumatic events/tragedies, psychical and/or psychological changes ***(being gravely ill for a long period of time, hormonal changes such as starting a menstrual cycle, menopause, pregnancy, etc.)***, NDE ***(near death experience)***, Etc.

When a person does experience an awakening, it can jolt the mind/body/spirit into a panic stage. This is often due to the heightened stages of each of our 5 senses ***(sight/sense/smell/taste/touch)*** that are activated during such events/experiences.

Some of the signs are a spiritual awakening are:

- Increased activity of psychic abilities, as well as other paranormal experiences ***(vivid dreams, out of body experiences, astral traveling, etc.)***
- Sensitivity to negative energies ***(whether in people, locations, objects, etc.)***
- Change in sleeping/eating habits ***(irregular sleep patterns, sleeping for a few hours then able to function all day without being tired, extreme thirst, cravings for certain foods, etc.)***
- Changes in interpersonal relationships with family/friends (***being unable to be around certain ones suddenly, etc.)***
- Instinctive primal behaviors ***(nesting/clearing out junk, desire to "return" back to basic way of life, sexual appetite changes/increases, etc.)***
- Unexplained panic attacks ***(with no logical explanation, etc.)***
- Psychical aches/pains ***(cramps, headaches, neck/shoulder ache, dizziness/vertigo, stomach/digestive issues, etc.)***
- Heightened sensitivity to fabrics ***(your skin's reaction to fabric in general: Suddenly being unable to wear something due to how it "feels" on your body, or desiring to have a certain fabric on your body because it "soothes" you, etc.)***
- Change in your hobbies/interests

- Overwhelming feelings of being connected to the energies of the world around you

When you feel these changes start to take place, it is normal to fear it, to question it, to question yourself and your level of sanity.

It is important that you not fight against these changed, but rather embrace and learn how to work with them as they occur. Let them flow as they occur within & around you.

Adapting to the changes will be beneficial while on your spirituality journey.

"There are no constraints on the human mind, no walls around the human spirit, no barriers to our progress except those we ourselves erect." - Ronald Reagan

STEP AWAY FROM THAT SPIRIT!

So you are a psychic medium. You are doing such a great job that you are devoted to it. Whenever free time you have, you are reading for your friends, family and clients. In between readings, you are researching, googling, studying, absorbing everything you possibly can absorb from all resources.

STOP.

Just like too many sodas can have an adverse effect on your body ***(teeth enamel can erode, kidneys become polluted, you can unnecessary weight, sugar increase, etc.)*** doing extensive back to back to back readings, studying, etc. can actually turn around and cause damage to your mind, body, spirit.

Professional psychic mediums understand that continuous spiritual work will take a toll on you overall:

- You feel lethargic
- You get body aches
- You feel as if you could sleep forever
- Can also cause minor bouts of depression ***(due to extensive & continuous spiritual work)***

The key here is balance:

- Try not to book more than 2 ***(3 at the most)*** clients in a day ***(or 1 gallery reading)***. This also goes for those who are now teaching spirituality
- Book your clients at least an hour apart of each other ***(allowing you time to eat/drink, stretch your body, recharge your own energy, etc.)***
- Designate a specific time of the day/evening where you step away ***(shut down)*** from readings, research, etc. and stick to it
- Give yourself a day off completely ***(this will allow your aura, your chakras and your body to heal and recoup overall)***
- Get Reiki ***(at least once a month)*** and/or a massage

- Listen to music ***(music is not only universal, but very therapeutic overall to the body & mind)***, move/dance to it, get lost in it

By establishing and maintaining a balance between your spirituality and the rest of your world, you will not only have a stronger connection to your spirituality overall ***(including the bond between your guides and those who have crossed over is strengthen as well)***, but you will feel fit & strong ***(emotionally, mentally, physically)***, thus giving you as more productive life.

DIFFERENCE BETWEEN READING FACES & READING SPIRITS

A person just starting out with giving mediumship readings is most often likely to begin by reading a face, rather than accessing and communicating with their spirit instead. Depending upon the face, they respond with "Looks like they could be a teacher", or the standard "looks open and friendly" (this is most often said with smiling faces), or "looks sad and lonely" ***(most often with faces that appear tired, etc.)***. Reading a spirit is far deeper than the surface expressions. It is literally the spirit of the face you are looking at.

To hone your skills as a psychic medium, you must push that surface level and delve deeply into their spirit. That vital connection between your guides, their spirit and yourself is the key to a productive reading.

In order to break through this surface level, you must connect with your spirit guides, as well as with the spirit that is connected with the face. Below are some steps to assist in getting you to that connection:

- Sit down in a quiet location ***(should be relatively free of clutter & distractions)***
- Regulate your breathing (take a deep breath in through your nose, hold for a count of 1-2-3, then exhale through your mouth. Repeat for a few times
- Shield yourself from outside disturbances ***(normal day to day white noise of family, pets, electronics, etc.)***
- Clear your mind from everything. Visualize yourself emptying out a filing cabinet ***(this is your mind)*** and tossing everything away in a large trash can. Then walk away from it and go sit down in a quiet area that you have created in your mind for yourself
- Briefly close your eyes and connect with your spirit guides. Be sure to ask for their assistance
- Once your guides are with you, open your eyes and focus on the image in front of you
- Ignore initial responses like "Looks like-" ***(teacher/sad/happy/friendly/angry/hard worker/nice grandmother/etc.)***

and delve deeper into the image, ***PAST*** their facial expression. This will take a few minutes ***(do not rush this!)***

- Once you have connected with their spirit, begin to communicate with them
- Some of the ways you can tell when you are communicating with a spirit in an image:
- You feel a slight vibration on and around you ***(some might call it a tingling sensation)***, especially in your third eye and crown chakras
- Your ears may ring/buzz some ***(this is from the spirit & your guides communicating with you)***
- Your chakras & your senses become heightened slightly and somewhat sensitive in nature ***(this is especially true about your heart Chakra, because it is the home of love, emotions, etc.)***

Now some of the ways you can receive messages from a spirit are as follows:

- Flashes of images ***(almost like instant camera style)***
- Movie ***(this is where it feels as if you are watching a movie on a big screen around you)***
- Whispers ***(sometimes shouts!)***
- Emotions/Smells/Sounds ***(where they project their specific feelings as way of a message)***

In many cases, you may experience what is known as Channeling ***(Trance Mediumship)*** during the connection.

Channeling ***(Trance Mediumship)*** is receiving a communication from specific spirits and either writing or speaking that communication as though the spirit itself is speaking.

It is always recommended that during this time, you keep a pen & paper handy to write/draw with while you are receiving spirit communication.

As their spirit begins to communicate with you and your guides, write down whatever information you are receiving ***(do not discount anything that you are***

receiving). Afterwards, thank them for coming forth and communicating with you and your guides.

Depending upon whether you have a client in front of you, or you are reading in a group, share ***(write if in online group)*** what you received from spirit.

As the session ends, be sure to break the connection between the spirit and your guides and yourself.

DEALING WITH EMOTIONS DURING READINGS

Whether we, as psychic mediums/mediums mean to or not, during readings, we will make a connection, give a message, etc. and this results in the sitter becoming emotional and crying.

For the new medium, this can be somewhat uncomfortable. Questions roll around in your mind:

- Do I hug them?
- Do I tell them it is ok?
- Do I ignore them crying?
- Should I stop the session or continue on but don't give messages that make them cry?

The answers are simple. Do what you feel is comfortable and what the sitter is comfortable with.

Understand that some might not be receptive to being touched or consoled, while some others actually would welcome a comforting hug.

What makes a successful reading session, is when all participants ***(the reader, the sitter(s)***, and those from the other side find solace and comfort.

This enables the sitter to move on ***(those from the other side as well in many cases)***.

Some tips on dealing with a sitter who is emotional and crying during a session:

- Pause for a moment, listen to them (doesn't matter if they are talking or not, sometimes just having a person "there" with you as you cry is often more powerful and healing than crying alone
- Reach out and touch their arm gently. Let them know you are there and present with them in the moment

- Smile, nod and listen, if they chose to share with you some of their memories at that moment
- Ask them if they want to take a brief break and get some water
- Reassure them that it is normal and ok that they get emotional and that there is nothing wrong with them, that tears are both healing and rejuvenating.

Special note for the readers who are also Empaths:

- Shield yourself
- Do not allow yourself to take on their emotions and memories. Those emotions and memories are theirs not yours. That is a violation of trust between sitter***(s)*** and reader and a line that should never, ever be crossed

When you end the session, be sure to offer to be there, should they want to talk again. Make sure that they are mentally & emotionally ok before you leave. Thank them for allowing you to share those moments and memories with them.

Always remember, that when you are asked to be a reader for a sitter(s), you are embracing not only their love ones messages, but their hearts.

That is a very intimate and personal space that not everyone is permitted to be included in.

Example of one of my readings with an older woman:

Client came in for a reading. She brought 2 images with her and offered her watch for me to wear during the reading, so the connection can be established.

During the reading, her father expressed his regret, and sorrow about an incident that occurred when she was 11 years old. He had kissed her on the mouth once during a family bar-b-que, while swimming in the family pool.

He expressed that there had been no other incidents previously, nor since, but that he felt so ashamed about that incident to where he made it a point never to go near her, never to hug her, never to do more than ***"love at a distance"*** and ***"be a hands off father figure."***

The clients face crumbled, as she buried her face in her hands and started to weep.

Several minutes went by silently. The father was present and silent, I also remained silent. I felt pain, grief and remorse from both sides ***(living and passed)***. I reached out and held her hands as her weeping turned into sobs.

During her this time, she explained that while the kiss felt wrong to her, she didn't feel like it was on purpose and couldn't understand why he shut himself off from her as a father overall and felt that he didn't love her ***(she also stated that he never made eye contact with her since that incident)***.

She stated that she also felt as if she was to blame for him not wanting to be around her, as the years went on. She further stated that it got so bad to where he didn't even walk her down the aisle at her wedding and that it crushed her because all she wanted was for her dad to love her as a daughter once more. She expressed gratitude for the apology but ached for the moments they missed as father/daughter.

While the client weeping and talking, I would pause for a few, then relay the messages from her father to her. Her father was apologizing for everything and asking her not to blame herself, that he never stopped loving and was proud of the woman she is, her but was so ashamed of that one incident to where he kept a distance so he wouldn't ***"screw her life up"***.

This was a bittersweet healing session for both sides.

Upon my leaving, I hugged the client, as I sent both of her parents with her. I felt drained. I knew in my heart that some healing had begun on both sides and I was honored enough to be present for that as a psychic medium.

DEBRIEFING AFTER A SESSION
(ESPECIALLY AN INTENSE SESSION)

Giving a psychic medium reading session is ***(usually)*** always productive and energetic. Both sides ***(the sitter and the reader)*** are filled with energy. This is a good thing. This in turn, will aide in the transference of messages from those who have crossed over.

But what does the psychic medium do with this energy after a session? What about if the session is an intense session and the energy is so intense, to where the psychic medium can feel as if they are on an overload of caffeine? What happens of the energy is not released? What are some of the drawbacks?

A strong connection to those who have crossed over can often be felt in a psychical sense such as:

- A buzzing in your ears
- That ***"rush"*** feeling as if you are on a roaring roller coaster
- ***"Bouncy"*** feeling ***(sometimes swinging your legs/feet under the table, etc.)***
- Tingling/tickling/fluttering in and around your chakras ***(especially your third eye & your solar plexius)***
- Some psychic mediums experience extreme thirst ***(or a drying of throat as well in some cases)***

During the session, the psychic medium can also feel whatever emotions, etc. they receive from those who have crossed over too ***(whether the messages come from pleasant and/or unpleasant emotions, etc.)***.

Once the session has ended some may experience:

- Hunger
- Thirsty
- Headache
- Sleepy/drained
- A "coating" on their skin and clothes

<u>A recommendation to assist in resolving these feelings are as follows:</u>

- Break the spiritual connection who those who have crossed over ***(this is extremely important)***
- Get a shower ***(first as hot as you can handle, suds up really good, then rinse off with warm, then give a blast of semi cold water and let it flow over your body)***
- Lean against the shower wall, close your eyes and simply exhale a few times as you imagine the emotions, spiritual connections, etc. flowing off of you and down into the drain
- Wear fresh clothing ***(do not wear the same clothing if possible & nothing tight/confining, etc.)***
- Smudge ***(sage)*** your area
- Light fresh incense ***(not the same fragrance as you had during the session if you had any)***
- Eat a light meal ***(take your time eating, enjoy each taste and flavor)***
- Listen to music ***(can be any type of music that appeals to you)***
- Do something fun ***(go for a brief walk, play a game, dance, etc.)***
- Go to bed early ***(some say that this is the most helpful)***

An additional note to those who utilize crystals & other props during the session, they also need to be ***"cleansed"*** and ***"rejuvenated"***.

<u>This can be done by the following process:</u>

- Gently wipe each tool/prop with a warm cloth
- Smudge/sage
- Stick in a freezer overnight ***(if possible)***
- Sit out in direct moonlight or sunlight for a few hours

The key here is to completely separate yourself from the session and give some much needed nourishment back to yourself ***(in every sense possible)***.

RECOGNISING & REMOVING EGO (Ego + messages = disaster)

As psychic mediums, it is our jobs ***(and pleasure)*** to relay messages from those who have crossed over, help out on criminal cases ***(for those who do)***, assist in a paranormal investigation, etc.

It can be quite rewarding to get the positive feedback that we are ***"right"*** about whatever impressions/visions/etc. we may receive. It can become addicting, getting those positive ***"Yes! You're right! OMG you are 100% spot on!"*** affirmations.

As the old saying goes ***"Too much of a good thing can kill you"***. So when it comes to giving readings ***(no matter what the capacity or format)*** it is really necessary to remove our egos from the equation entirely.

Signs that your ego is over shadowing your session:

- You have this need to constantly be right
- You have this hunger for feedback and when the information you relay isn't correct or the sitter cannot validate it, you become irritable and short in your responses
- You become argumentive
- You start to ***(not only)*** feel angry, but your tone & body language changes to a confrontational stance

This can be especially true whenever there is a team of psychic mediums, who all gather together to work on one session.

Sometimes, during a group reading ***(where there is more than one psychic medium present and reading, etc.)***, jealousy gets mixed in with ego and the result is chaos and argument: Jealousy + Ego = Chaos/argument.

Case example:

Three psychic mediums attend a paranormal investigation at a private residence. The paranormal team leader walks through the residence with the psychic mediums and documents their findings.

At the end of the session, an argument erupts:

Team Leader: Ok guys here we are, let's walk into the living room first-

Psychic medium 1: I'm sensing a little girl in here. Playful. Sweet nature. Something wrong with her leg.

Psychic medium 2: I'm sensing it is her right leg but more of a birth defect like. But yes she is a gentle soul.

Psychic medium 3: Yeah I got the kid, but something else too. Can't place my finger on it. Can we keep walking please?

The Team Leader takes them around the kitchen and into one of the bedrooms:

Psychic medium 1: Ok. Yes. Here is where the little girl was beaten & raped. It was her father. He was a horrible man. A drunk. It went on for years. She killed herself in this room. So much sadness.

Psychic medium 2: No I'm not getting any of that. I do get that she was in this room quite a bit. She was really sad and lonely. But I'm not getting anything else like what you did. Sorry.

Psychic medium 3: I get that this is where the little girl stayed mostly. She feels isolated to me. As if she couldn't move....as if she was being held down or tied to something. Strange.

The Team Leader wraps up the investigation with the 3 psychic mediums, then takes the rest of the team in for their investigation.

Later an argument can be heard from nearby the vehicles between the Team Leader & psychic medium 1:

Psychic medium 1: I SAID I WAS RIGHT!!! I KNOW I AM RIGHT!!! YOU CAN'T TELL ME I AM EVER WRONG I HAVE BEEN DOING THIS FOR A LONG TIME AND I KNOW WHAT I KNOW DAMMIT!

Team Leader: You need to calm down. You were wrong with the details and that is ok-

Psychic medium 1: I SAID I WAS RIGHT!!! I DON'T CARE WHAT ANYONE SAYS!!! I HAVE MORE EXPERIENCE THAN THOSE OTHER WANNABE PSYCHICS!!! BUT NEVER MIND BECAUSE I AM LEAVING THIS TEAM NOW!!! YOU JUST LOST YOURSELF A TRUE PSYCHIC MEDIUM!!!

He gets into his car and speeds off in a ranting huff, leaving the Team Leader shaking his head and shuffling everyone back to the side so he can regroup his team.

As it has been demonstrated here, ego was destructive. Anytime ego comes into play during a session, it needs to be escorted out quickly or the results could leave an ugly (and lasting) impression.

If you come to a point where you feel that your ego is starting to appear or you become jealous over something or someone, you should immediately separate yourself from the session and ask your guides and yourself why are you feeling these emotions? Ask your guides to offer you some assistance ***(talk to them directly)***.

If after a few moments, you can't seem to control your ego and/or jealousy under control, then you should separate yourself entirely from the area, while you ask yourself:

- WHY am I feeling this jealousy and anger so much?
- WHY do I have to be right all the time?

Being a psychic medium is a beautiful gift. But always remember that even though we have been blessed with this beautiful gift, we are still human first and foremost. This means that we will make mistakes ***(sometimes even during the sessions)***.

On the note about working with other psychic mediums and/or other team members:

It is vital that we always remain professional and conduct ourselves as professionals whenever we are out in a public ***(dealing with the public)*** setting.

Bottom line, you can be the best psychic medium out there, but if your professional reputation is tarnished by your ego, jealousy and argumentive personality, then you can close your business doors now, because all it takes is for 1 or 2 clients who witnessed you at your worst to impact your client flow.

Some tips to help separate your ego:

- Understand that whatever messages you are receiving from those who have crossed over is not about you. You are the vessel ***(the person in the middle between those who have crossed over and the living)***
- If you are working on a team ***(especially with other psychic mediums),*** understand that not everyone is going to have the same ***"vision"*** and/or ***"impression"*** as you. Be welcome and receptive to other psychic mediums responses and information ***(perhaps they can tap into something that you are simply unable to tap into during that session)***
- Understand & accept that you will be wrong occasionally ***(NO psychic medium is EVER 100% correct 100% of the time)***
- Prior to going into a session (whether solo or galley session or working with a team on a case), seek the assistance of your guides to help you remove your ego and ask them to give you clues when your ego starts to roar up during sessions ***(your guides are with you to advise and to work with you, so work with them)***

POINTS TO REMEMBER WHEN GIVING ONLINE READINGS

With virtually anything & everything can be performed online these days, it is no wonder that online mediumship reading is preferred by many. Look at some of the perks:

- Don't have to leave your house
- Really don't have to get dressed ***(unless you are skyping, then please wear something!)***
- Saves wear & tear ***(not to mention gas!)*** on your vehicle
- Whether you are new to mediumship or an experienced medium, reading online clearly has it's benefits. However, there are some drawbacks.

Excessive and/or prolonged computer usage can create physical & mental strain on you. Some warning signs:

- Muscle tightness/stiffness ***(from sitting in one position or hunched over your monitor for long periods)***
- Back aches ***(posture, sitting in a wooden chair, little to no support, etc.)***
- Headaches
- Computer Vision Syndrome ***(strain and sometimes eye pain from over working the eyes/ eye muscles)***

<u>Some ways you can prevent and/or counteract these symptoms are as follows:</u>

- Be sure to get up from your seat at least once an hour, for just a few moments ***(actually once every half hour is preferred but sometimes during a reading you simply cannot get away that often)***, stretch your body, grab something to drink, eat, etc.
- Be sure your seat is comfortable but firm and your back ***(from the lower to mid/upper)*** is fully supported, arm rests is also a big plus!
- Sit your monitor in a well light room ***(reduces eye strain)***
- Be sure that your monitor light is set to a comfortable level

- Divert your eyes from the screen occasionally during readings so that your eyes can focus on something that is less harsh and direct ***(a window, pictures on your wall, etc.)***
- Wiggle your legs under the desk ***(as kids we are taught to be still, but as an adult wiggling our legs assists in keeping the blood and oxygen flowing through our bodies, so in the end our muscles aren't do tight, we don't feel so "wore out")***
- Place a cool beanie bag over your eyes for a moment or two at the end of your readings

In today's society, many, many people ***(ranging from young to old)*** are experiencing computer-related eye issues.

Be smart. Just like being in an airplane, place the oxygen mask on yourself first before helping others in need.

Now spiritually, be sure to give yourself a break in between readings ***(even if for only a few moments)***. If you don't then not only are you carrying over previous energy from last reading, but you are overloading your guides, as well as yourself.

UNEXPECTED TRANCES
(WHAT ARE THEY & HOW TO DEAL WITH THEM)

A trance is an altered state of half-consciousness. This altered state can be triggered by external stimuli ***(music, energy, people, places, energy, etc.)***

<u>There are basically 3 levels of trance:</u>

- Light
- Full
- Heavy/Deep

Trances can be induced or appear unexpectedly with little to no control over it.

<u>For psychics & psychics mediums, this can feel like a whirlwind of:</u>

"OMG's", mixed with "WTH ***(what the hell)", as your mind tries to make sense of the mass amount of information that is rolling over you like a raging Tsunami wave (even the most experienced psychics and psychic mediums have this here and there within their journeys)***.

A "***<u>light trance</u>***" is usually soft and gentle like a daydream. It is soothing, comforting, peaceful. Your mind and body feel as if you are being comforted by "***warm fuzzies***". Many experience this level during Reiki, Yoga or meditation.

A "***<u>Full Trance</u>***" is heavier. Your body feels heavy, you get somewhat dizzy, sleepy, as if you are being sedated or hypnotized. Images from your mind's eye can begin to appear, your breathing is somewhat labored. Also any sharp (unexpected) sounds can jolt you and feel as if they are slicing through your body.

A "***<u>Heavy/Deep</u>***" trance is the deepest of all trances. You feel completely submerged in a sea of visions, sounds, & sensations. Your outside body becomes heavy, as if you are being held down and simply cannot move, while your body on the inside feels as if jolts of electricity is being run through your organs ***(your heart beats wildly sometimes, your stomach might flip flop, etc.)***

During this stage, your breathing is very labored ***(some might feel a ringing/tingling in their ears/head)***, your mind is very focused. At this state, while you are very much aware of the moment, you, might not remember very much of the details afterwards.

For psychic mediums, an unexpected trance usually comes in at the full to heavy/deep trance stage. The mass amount of images, mixed with swirls of information can actually feel as if you are in a vortex of swirling energies. Your mouth speaks words, relaying information, but it sounds as if you are outside of your own mind and body, etc.

While this state might feel as if it lasts for extended periods of time ***(some may feel as if it lasts hour or more)***, it reality it can last several minutes ***(there is some speculation that time doesn't exist in this level of altered state of consciousness)***. When this happens unexpectedly, it is recommended to accept it, allow it to flow through you ***(as long as you are in a safe place, if you are driving please do NOT engage in this, find a safe place to pull off and allow it to continue OR find the strength to push it down until you can better receive the trance information)***

Afterwards, you can feel an array of emotions and body aches, such as:

- Shortness of breath
- Sweaty/shaky hand and/or palms
- Exhaustion (both mental & physical)
- Sleepy/tired
- "Spent"
- Mild to dull headache
- Muscle ache
- Mild disorientation
- Thirsty

It is always recommended to keep 2 things nearby while in a trance state, as well as coming out of a trance state:

- Digital recorder
- Glass of water ***(some may opt for wine)***

The digital recorder is handy to record your words while in trance, while the glass of water ***(or wine)*** helps ground and center you upon exiting the trance.

As a last step upon exiting the trance, it is recommended to get a cool refreshing shower, while imaging rays of soft, golden light flowing over your body, helping it to center, ground and heal ***(during this stage some may opt to also include a sprig or two of Eucalyptus to their showerhead and allow the water to flow over it and onto the body as well)***.

Afterwards it is recommended that you eat a small ***(light)*** meal ***(and attempt to get a decent night sleep or a catnap if possible)***, to assist in rebuilding your energy.

******NOTICE*** If symptoms persist then consider seeking medical advice and/or attention promptly***

WHEN TO SHARE SENSITIVE INFORMATION (AND HOW TO HANDLE THE SELF BLAME GAME)

One of the main questions students most often ask is ***"When do I know it is ok to share sensitive information with a person?"***

First, you should gauge whether or not the person in question would be open to receive this form of sensitive information, in addition to, if they aren't, then ***3 questions need to be answered***:

- Is this person important enough in my life to share this information regardless of their views and opinions of psychic mediums?
- How important is this information exactly? Is it life changing?
- Are you prepared for whatever is given to you as a response from this person?

AUTHORS PERSONAL STORY

Two years ago, my guides gave me a ***"Practice what you preach"*** lesson one day. My husband was away on an overseas deployment and I was helping our yard guy, Stan, put in a new door on our back porch. Within a few moments, a vision hit me. I saw Stan falling out of a huge tree, with a running chainsaw.

Needless to say it unnerved me. Stan had been working for us for almost a year and I dearly loved this man. He was quirky, outspoken to a fault, very ***"Northerner"*** as opposed to my southern style and while at times we clashed somewhat on opinions, we definitely had formed a strong bond of friendship.

Anyhow, I felt a sense of panic as a wave of vision flowed over me again, to where I had to lean against the wall and close my eyes for a moment. Stan, being Stan, thought I needed to get something to drink ***(it was rather hot outside)***.

I went and got a glass of water then returned to watch him for a second. Then took a deep breath and decided to share with him what I saw and hoped that he listened to me.

What transpired was my getting chewed out up and down by this 64 year old man. Scolding me for believing in ***"That poppycock nonsense that only a child would believe in."***

To say that I felt as if I was a child at that moment was a great understatement. For a few awkward moments, there was an uncomfortable silence that hung in the air. I quickly made an excuse of having to go do laundry, in order to get away. Just before leaving, I gave last plea of ***"Stan regardless of your views please do not climb any trees today with a chainsaw!"*** then asked him if he wanted me to get him anything while I was out.

He half barked at me that he was too busy with my porch stairs that he built himself and my plants to be messing around with any chainsaws that day.

As I started to leave he half waved at me and asked that I get him a pop ***(soda)***.

I lingered at some stores after my laundry, dreading going home and facing Stan, fearing he would still chastise me on some level. Basically I was feeling as if I was a child.

I got home right around dusk, I didn't see Stan. I marveled at the door and my new steps, while talking with my dog groomer (who also was a good friend of mine and who also thought psychic stuff was a waste of time and only meant for idiots) on my cell, when this elderly woman came up to my fence and asked if my name was Sue and if I knew Stan.

I nodded and asked why then dropped my phone as I heard "There has been an accident. Stan was trimming my tree on top of my roof and he slipped and fell with the chainsaw."

I felt as if I had been punched in the stomach, as I asked if he fell on the chainsaw. He had not, but wasn't responsive. He had been flown to Miami trauma and that nobody knew anything else at that time.

I went back and grabbed my phone. I called my friend back and told her what happened. Her response was ***"Ok that is terrible but it isn't like you shoved him off the roof right?"***

I won't lie, that question shot through me like a bullet. I made an excuse to get off the phone and quickly went inside to sit down. The only thing that went through my mind over and over was the question ***"It isn't like you shoved him of the roof right?"***

Stan stayed in ICU for 3 months. His heart has stopped twice during the flight. He had broken his neck and would forever be paralyzed and relying on a respirator.

My husband soon came home and after I broke down and cried about what happened, he said we needed to go visit Stan. I refused. I panicked. ***What if he remembered that day and blamed me? What if he gets so angry at me that he strokes out and dies in front of me? And the biggest question that refused to leave my mind "Was this really my fault? Did I unwittingly suggest to him that he would fall?***

My husband, being of logic, but understanding my world now ***(after 20+ years)***, forced me to go. He said we owed it to Stan and that it would be beneficial for all of us.

The drive to the hospital is 4 hours each direction ***(we live in the islands)***, on the way there, I begged my guides for strength and guidance. All I got back was "***Breathe***"

We arrived at the hospital and made our way to his room. There was a sign in sheet there, gloves, cape, etc. His family was there as well ***(his daughters and his mother, who was in a wheelchair)***. And there was Stan, hooked up to machines and I.V.'s.

His family greeted us and we chatted for a few moments outside in the hallways, each taking a few moments to go see him.

When it was my time, I grabbed my husband hand and asked him to go with me. I was literally shaking and I couldn't decide if I was going to burst into tears, throw up, or faint ***(knowing my luck, it probably would have been all three if I had to go in alone)***.

We went in and Stan saw me. He gave me a soft smile and motioned with his eyes for me to come closer. Gently I did and leaned in to say hi to him and ask how he was. He said he was fine, just being lazy. He made a joke! I felt my spirits go up somewhat hearing his response and giggled. I then asked him if he remembered anything about that day. He closed his eyes and mouthed "No." A deep sense of relief covered me like a warm blanket as I fought to keep the tears from flowing.

We stayed for a few more minutes, then said our goodbyes and left. In the safety of our car, I broke down and sobbed like a child. I felt a buffet table of emotions, ranging from remorse, guilt, anger, confusion to exhaustion and relief.

I decided not to do any readings, or teach anyone until I could effectively process the accident, my role and my responses from everything.

We made it to see Stan twice more, then one night, as I was coming home from a late night photo shoot, I saw and heard Stan in my backyard, cutting some wood, telling me that he was going to fix my front steps rail then work on my grass. I knew that was a visit from him. I smiled and nodded as I went inside my home.

Later that next morning I received a call from a friend telling me that Stan has passed away the night before.

I saw that elderly woman once more after learning of Stan's death and asked her if she was ok and how did she know Stan. She explained that she was a widow and Stan would often pop over to help her out. On that particular day, she noticed him working on my back porch and asked if he could come over to trim a few trees for her. He said yes after he finished up with my new stairs he built.

I viewed this as a learning experience from my guides. Although in all honestly, I wished they had chosen a different path to enlighten me.

If you were to ask me if I would change anything in my telling Stan about my vision, I would say no. I felt then as I do now, that it was important enough and he was important enough for me to risk everything and warn him.

THE IMPORTANCE OF CONTINUOUS SPIRITUAL EDUCATION

The biggest fact to always keep in mind as a psychic medium is that you never stop learning while on your spiritual journey.

A common fear amongst many psychic mediums ***(novice and seasoned)*** is that if you don't use your abilities constantly or you stop learning ***(or in some cases take a break from it for one reason or another)***; you actually could lose your abilities.

What actually happens is that your abilities become dormant. Now while this is frightening on a very personal level, it is not permanent by any means.

But this drives home a valid point of continuous education while on your spiritual journey.

Some areas that you, as a psychic medium must always keep educating yourself on are as follows:

- Auras
- Astral Projection
- Psychic abilities ***(all of them)***
- Reiki/Meditation techniques
- Shielding/grounding techniques
- Fresh and new ways to connect with spirits
- Latest scientific discoveries within the studies of psychic abilities
- Latest healthcare discoveries

Now while majority of those areas are directly connected with your spiritual journey, the healthcare discoveries is just as important. This is because it is important to keep your mind and body in tip top shape and fit at all times.

If your mind and body is not working at their optimum level, your psychic mediumship abilities could ***(and often do)*** suffer.

Some of the ways you can keep you mind sharp:

- Puzzles ***(online, or those you can psychically put together, virtual puzzles, crossword puzzles, games, etc.)***
- Reading ***(all types of books, pick one topic you know nothing about and search for some books on it, learn about it, take it all in, see how it relates to you and your spiritual journey)***
- Learn a new hobby ***(gardening, painting, drawing, etc.)*** from the basics to the most advanced

By constantly learning and keeping your mind and body fit, your spiritual journey only advances and your awakening process proceeds smoother.

This results in you having a stronger connection not only to your psychic abilities, but to the spirits who have crossed over, as well as your guides and those entities on other realms.

PSYCHICS, MEDIUMS, PSYCHIC MEDIUMS & THE LAW

As you explore your spirituality path, you learn about how to take care of yourself ***(your aura/chakras/overall well-being/etc.)***, you learn how to communicate with your guides, as well as those in the afterlife, etc. What isn't thoroughly discussed or review extensively is the legal system and you, as a psychic, medium, or a psychic medium.

Every person who enters the world of psychics, mediums, psychic mediums, has to possess the basic understanding of the legal system and how it relates to what they are doing ***(even if it is for a hobby)***. Ignorance in the eyes of the law is not an acceptable defense in today's courtroom.

Areas that psychics, mediums and psychic mediums should research, understand and be educated about are as follows:

- BUSINESSES LICENSES
- MEDICAL ADVICE/DIAGNOISES
- SLANDER/LIABILITY
- LAW ENFORCEMENT ***(CRIMES, ETC.)*** & ADMISSABLE EVIDENCE

BUSINESS LICENSES:

Each state varies in their requirement for operating a psychic business ***(even if you are running your business as a hobby, be sure to research your states definition of "hobby" under running a business to see if you fall within that category)***.

MOST states ***(and counties)*** will require a psychic, medium and/or a psychic medium to have a valid business license. This includes their DBA (doing business as) and their tax I.D. number ***(most often their social security number)***.

In ***SOME*** areas ***(such as Southern Nevada/Las Vegas)***, you must have a criminal background check ***(and be fingerprinted)*** in order to obtain a psychic arts license ***(there are some loopholes and exceptions within this requirement, so diligent research is required on your part)***.

When traveling to a different state to perform at an event, it is advisable for you to contact that states business license department as a soon as possible to verify whether or not you need a state or county license/permit for them as well

When in doubt, it is always encouraged that you contact your local state and county business license department and speak to them directly.

The penalties for operating a business ***(as defined by your state and county)*** without a license are steep, ranging from fines/penalties to possible jail time.

MEDICAL ADVICE/DIAGNOISES:

There comes a time when all psychics, mediums and/or psychic mediums will be privy to intimate medical conditions/issues within a certain person. The dilemma is to whether or not to inform that person of what you "feel".

While each state has their own individual regulations that pertain to the practice of medicine, generally one is considered to be practicing medicine if they are:

- Diagnose a medical condition
- Attempt to treat a medical condition ***(including surgery)***
- Offer medicines, etc.
- Giving medical examinations
- Offering medical advice

Some of the areas that is NOT included:

- Selling books pertaining to medicine, nutrition, self-help, etc. & vitamins
- Healing (Reiki, yoga, meditation, etc.)

If you ***"feel"*** a certain medical condition applies to a certain person and you chose to inform that person of what you feel, understand that you are then placing yourself in the category of ***"diagnosing a medical condition"***. This can be interpreted as ***"Practicing medicine without a license"***.

You then risk liability charges, as well as county/state charges of:

- Operating a business with no business license or insurance
- Federal charges including felony criminal charges:
- Practicing without a medical license
- Criminal manslaughter (involuntarily or voluntarily)
- Not to mention personal civil lawsuits from the person and/or their surviving family members for:
- Loss of wages/incomes

- Financial, physical, or psychological harm

SLANDER/LIABILITY

<u>Slander</u> is defined as any false statements/verbiage spoken about a certain person that stands the risk of causing reputation damage.

<u>Liable</u> is defined as any statement or reference given in writing about a person that stands the risk of reputation damage.

Whenever a psychic, medium and/or a psychic medium gives a reading about an absent third party ***(spouse, partner, friend, business acquaintance, etc.)***, they stand the risk of slander/liability backwash if the information they receive is presented within a negative and/or unflattering manner.

****

<u>Case example:</u>

Psychic: Hi! Thank you for booking me today! How can I help you?
Client: I want to know about my husband and my best friend. They have been sneaky for this last month and I want to know what is going on.
Psychic: Ok, give me your wedding ring and let me focus (closes their eyes for a few moments, then opens and begins to talk): Is your friend Barbara?
Client: Yes.
Psychic: Is your husband Keith?
Client: Yes. What do you see them doing!
Psychic ***(closes their eyes and focuses some more then opens and talks)***: I'm seeing a large boat, like a cruise ship and now I see them in a hotel room, walking around it, looking at the view outside on the balcony. They look happy. Now I see them in a jewelry store, looking at something-
Client ***(upset):*** Oh my god! Are they having an affair with each other?!
Psychic ***(leans over and hands the ring back to the client and says)***: Yes. I know this for a fact they are having an affair. I'm so sorry but it is better you know this now and leave them both! You deserve better! Once a cheater ***ALWAYS*** a cheater!

The session ends with the client going home in tears, packing her clothes and leaving. While on her way out of the area, she contacts her attorney to begin divorce proceedings.

Later it was discovered that the husband enlisted the help of his wife's best friend to help create a romantic weekend get-away on a cruise ship that also included an overnight hotel stay at a 5 star hotel and a new diamond necklace they both picked out.

****

It is vital that if you, as a psychic medium and/or a psychic medium ***never*** attempt to read a third party without their consent ***(which is not advisable to many, however some elect to do so),*** that you refrain from accusing that third party of unflattering activities.

To do so willingly, is to run the risk of potential slander/liability charges ***(which whether they hold up in a court of law or not doesn't matter because by that point the local media would have gotten the scoop on this and you just might find yourself on their radar for "news".)***

LAW ENFORCEMENT (CRIMES, ETC.) & ADMISSABLE EVIDENCE:

The allure of assisting the police in a case is a strong drug for some psychics & psychic mediums. There's the thrill of "***seeing***" the crime as it unfolds in your mind, the feel of being "***important & needed***" by the law enforcement personnel in a certain case.

The one thing to understand is that ***YOU*** do not solve the case. ***YOU*** are a tool, in which the police department has elected to utilize because they are out of leads and have nowhere else to turn to. ***YOU*** are their last resort.

While there are some law enforcement agencies ***(whether inside certain departments, etc.)*** that do utilize psychics and psychic mediums, there are far more law enforcement agencies that will not and ***DO NOT*** actively entertain the notion of using a psychic, psychic medium at all Ever.

There are 2 reasons why they will not and do not ever use them:

- For every "valid" psychic, psychic medium worth their grain of salt, there are ***(at the minimum)*** 20+ self-proclaimed psychics and psychic mediums who are frauds & fakes. They are in it for the $$$ and glory ***(ego)*** only
- Any and ***ALL*** information given to law enforcement by a psychic, psychic medium is ***NOT*** allowed to be submitted in court ***(prosecuting attorneys simply cannot include whatever information from the psychic, psychic medium as "admissible evidence")***

So why even bother contacting law enforcement about a vison you feel might have some connection to a case they are working on?

Because you might be able to give some valid insight to provide to them, this could result in more productive leads on their side, thus solving the case.

Remember though, ***YOU*** do ***NOT*** solve a criminal case***. LAW ENFOREMENT*** does. But that doesn't mean that you cannot be used as a tool in their investigation ***(ONLY when they are open to the concept of using a psychic, psychic medium)***.

AUTHOR'S BIO:

Sue M. Swank was born in Washington, D.C. and raised in Richmond, Virginia.

As a natural born psychic medium, her gifts came to her within her childhood ***(as well as her paranormal encounters with the afterlife)***.

While growing up in a home where there was an unsolved murder, she began to relay details of the crime to her parents and explained that they came from the woman who had died in the home.

Sue has learned through years of experience, how to fine tune her abilities ***(Empath abilities with strengths in psychometry/precognition & retrocognition mixed with her psychic mediumship)*** and expand on them.

Over the course of the years, she has also expanded her professional field to include working on cold/unsolved cases with law enforcement and teaching psychic mediumship.

Currently, Sue resides in the Florida Keys with her Husband and their German Shepherd dog, "Chance" and enjoys a very full life as a professional photographer, psychic medium and paranormal investigator.

Sue is available for psychic mediumship readings via phone, internet ***(email/skype/etc.)*** and of course, in person.

Sue Swank also offers "online courses" on various subjects all related to psychic mediumship. Ask her for her current schedule.

You can contact her through these social media outlets:

WEBPAGE: http://sueswank.weebly.com

FACEBOOK: https://www.facebook.com/psychicmediumsuesank

TWITTER: https://twitter.com/sueswank

EMAIL: keywestswank@aol.com

91348870R00062

Made in the USA
Middletown, DE
29 September 2018